Preface

My goal for putting together the four ⟨ order is to have a better understanding of Jesus the Christ while he was physically v.... .... writing begins with John 1:1 and ends, after the beginning of the Church, in Acts 2:47.

I was saved in 1978 at the age of thirty-three. Ever since that time I have been under the impression that some of the events in the Gospels are one in the same even though they are written different. I know there are no mistakes or contradictions in the Gospels and when I started this project I came to a different understanding of some of these events. I now believe each of the four Gospels can stand alone but still fit together providing we understand some of these events, even though they seem to be the same, are not, like the calling of the disciples and the Sermons on the Mount. It is believed by some writers that Matthew 5:1 to 7:29 and Luke 6:17-49 are two separate events.

When more than one Gospel recorded an event, or teaching I used the one with the most information and, when needed, I used verses from the other Gospels to provide more information and a more accurate account of what was being said or done.

I have included notes at the end of this writing to help you understand the scripture they are related to.

There are certain facts you need to consider when reading the Gospels.

(a) None of the four Gospels gives us a total accounting of all the events and teachings of Jesus during his earthly ministry. Putting the Gospels together in chronological order, with the events and teachings as they happened gives us a better understanding of his life and ministry. John 21:25 says: Jesus did many other things as well. If every one of them were written down, I suppose that even the whole world would not have room for books that would be written.

(b) The Gospels were not written in verse and paragraph form or in chronological order. They were written as one long sentence. When I put this writing together I used the different events in the Gospels, like the arrest of John the Baptist, and compared them with the same event in the other Gospels to determine what came before them and what came after them. I also have four other

Harmonies, which none of them totally agree with each other, that I used to help determine the chronological order of each event.

(c) The men who wrote the Gospels were told to do so through the inspiration of the Holy Spirit. 2nd Timothy 3:16-17 says: All scripture is God-breathed and is useful for teaching, rebuking, correcting and training in righteousness, so that the man of God may be thoroughly equipped for every good work.

(d) There is more we do not know, than what we do know about the ministry of Jesus, but what we do not know will never be inconsistent with what we do know.

Knowing about Jesus is not enough to provide you with eternal life in heaven with him. You have to know him personally as your Saviour and believe he is who he says he is and that he is the only truth, life and way. There is no other! John 14:5-7

If you already know him I hope this writing will give you a better understanding of his life and ministry.

If you do not know him I pray that you will accept the free gift of Salvation that he has already provided for you. He loves you so much that he willingly laid down his life for you on a Roman Cross and on the third day he rose from the dead which proved he is who he said he is.

Paul W. Auman Sr.

aumansr@gmail.com

Completed: February 16, 2018

Note: The words of Jesus are written in *Italic*

Acknowledgements

I would like to thank my wife Patricia for her love, support, encouragement, and being patient with me for all the time it took out of our schedule to put this book together.

I would also like to thank Pastor Tim Halbfoerster, our Lead pastor at "River of God Church" in Enola, Pa. for his help and encouragement. Without his support this book would have never been published.

I would also like to thank Pastor Rafe Sanderson, our Youth pastor, for his guidance, support, and help with the publishing of this book.

This is His Story

The Word Became Flesh
John 1:1-5

1 In the beginning was the Word, and the Word was with God, and the Word was fully God. 2 The Word was with God in the beginning. 3 All things were created by him, and apart from him not one thing was created that has been created. 4 In him was life, and the life was the light of mankind. 5 And the light shines on in the darkness, but the darkness has not mastered it.

John 1: 9-14

9 The true light, who gives light to everyone, was coming into the world. 10 He was in the world, and the world was created by him, but the world did not recognize him. 11 He came to what was his own, but his own people did not receive him. 12 But to all who have received him – those who believe in his name – he has given the right to become God's children 13 – children not born by human parents or by human desire or a husband's decision, but by God.

14 Now the Word became flesh and took up residence among us. We saw his glory – the glory of the one and only, full of grace and truth, who came from the Father.

John the Baptist Foretold
John 1: 6-8

6 A man came, sent from God, whose name was John. 7 He came as a witness to testify about the light, so that everyone might believe through him. 8 He himself was not the light, but he came to testify about the light.

Mark 1:2-3

2 As it is written in Isaiah the prophet, "Look, I am sending my messenger ahead of you, who will prepare your way, 3 the voice of one shouting in the wilderness, 'Prepare the way for the Lord, make his paths straight.'"

The Birth of John the Baptist
-In the Temple at Jerusalem-
Luke 1:5-25

5 During the reign of Herod king of Judea, there lived a priest named Zechariah who belonged to the priestly division of Abijah, and he had a wife named Elizabeth, who was a descendant of

Aaron. 6 They were both righteous in the sight of God, following all the commandments and ordinances of the Lord blamelessly. 7 But they did not have a child, because Elizabeth was barren, and they were both very old.

8 Now while Zechariah was serving as priest before God when his division was on duty, 9 he was chosen by lot, according to the custom of the priesthood, to enter the holy place of the Lord and burn incense. 10 Now the whole crowd of people were praying outside at the hour of the incense offering. 11 An angel of the Lord, standing on the right side of the altar of incense, appeared to him. 12 And Zechariah, visibly shaken when he saw the angel, was seized with fear. 13 But the angel said to him, "Do not be afraid, Zechariah, for your prayer has been heard, and your wife Elizabeth will bear you a son; you will name him John. 14 Joy and gladness will come to you, and many will rejoice at his birth, 15 for he will be great in the sight of the Lord. He must never drink wine or strong drink, and he will be filled with the Holy Spirit, even before his birth. 16 He will turn many of the people of Israel to the Lord their God. 17 And he will go as forerunner before the Lord in the spirit and power of Elijah, to turn the hearts of the fathers back to their children and the disobedient to the wisdom of the just, to make ready for the Lord a people prepared for him."

18 Zechariah said to the angel, "How can I be sure of this? For I am an old man, and my wife is old as well." 19 The angel answered him, "I am Gabriel, who stands in the presence of God, and I was sent to speak to you and to bring you this good news. 20 And now, because you did not believe my words, which will be fulfilled in their time, you will be silent, unable to speak, until the day these things take place."

21 Now the people were waiting for Zechariah, and they began to wonder why he was delayed in the holy place. 22 When he came out, he was not able to speak to them. They realized that he had seen a vision in the holy place, because he was making signs to them and remained unable to speak. 23 When his time of service was over, he went to his home.

24 After some time his wife Elizabeth became pregnant, and for five months she kept herself in seclusion. She said, 25 "This is what the Lord has done for me at the time when he has been gracious to me, to take away my disgrace among people."

The Foretold Birth Announcement of Jesus the Messiah

26 In the sixth month of Elizabeth's pregnancy, the angel Gabriel was sent by God to a town of Galilee called Nazareth, 27 to a virgin engaged to a man whose name was Joseph, a descendant of David, and the virgin's name was Mary. 28 The angel came to her and said, "Greetings, favored one, the Lord is with you!" 29 But she was greatly troubled by his words and began to wonder about the meaning of this greeting. 30 So the angel said to her, "Do not be afraid, Mary, for you have found favor with God! 31 Listen: You will become pregnant and give birth to a son, and you will name him Jesus. 32 He will be great, and will be called the Son of the Most High, and the Lord God will give him the throne of his father David. 33 He will reign over the house of Jacob forever, and his kingdom will never end." 34 Mary said to the angel, "How will this be, since I have not had sexual relations with a man?" 35 The angel replied, "The Holy Spirit will come upon you, and the power of the Most High will overshadow you. Therefore the child to be born will be holy; he will be called the Son of God.

36 "And look, your relative Elizabeth has also become pregnant with a son in her old age – although she was called barren, she is now in her sixth month! 37 For nothing will be impossible with God." 38 So Mary said, "Yes, I am a servant of the Lord; let this happen to me according to your word." Then the angel departed from her.

Mary Visits Elizabeth
-Hill Country of Judea-
Luke 1:39-45

39 In those days Mary got up and went hurriedly into the hill country, to a town of Judah, 40 and entered Zechariah's house and greeted Elizabeth. 41 When Elizabeth heard Mary's greeting, the baby leaped in her womb, and Elizabeth was filled with the Holy Spirit. 42 She exclaimed with a loud voice, "Blessed are you among women, and blessed is the child in your womb! 43 And who am I that the mother of my Lord should come and visit me? 44 For the instant the sound of your greeting reached my ears, the baby in my womb leaped for joy. 45 And blessed is she who believed that what was spoken to her by the Lord would be fulfilled."

Mary's Song of Praise
-Hill Country of Judea-
Luke 1:46-56

46 And Mary said, "My soul exalts the Lord, 47 and my spirit has begun to rejoice in God my Savior, 48 because he has looked upon the humble state of his servant. For from now on all generations will call me blessed, 49 because he who is mighty has done great things for me, and holy is his name; 50 from generation to generation he is merciful to those who fear him. 51 He has demonstrated power with his arm; he has scattered those whose pride wells up from the sheer arrogance of their hearts. 52 He has brought down the mighty from their thrones, and has lifted up those of lowly position; 53 he has filled the hungry with good things, and has sent the rich away empty. 54 He has helped his servant Israel, remembering his mercy, 55 as he promised to our ancestors, to Abraham and to his descendants forever." 56 So Mary stayed with Elizabeth about three months and then returned to her home.

The Birth of John the Baptist
-Hill Country of Judea-
Luke: 1:57-66

57 Now the time came for Elizabeth to have her baby, and she gave birth to a son. 58 Her neighbors and relatives heard that the Lord had shown great mercy to her, and they rejoiced with her.

59 On the eighth day they came to circumcise the child, and they wanted to name him Zechariah after his father. 60 But his mother replied, "No! He must be named John." 61 They said to her, "But none of your relatives bears this name." 62 So they made signs to the baby's father, inquiring what he wanted to name his son. 63 He asked for a writing tablet and wrote, "His name is John." And they were all amazed. 64 Immediately Zechariah's mouth was opened and his tongue released, and he spoke, blessing God. 65 All their neighbors were filled with fear, and throughout the entire hill country of Judea all these things were talked about. 66 All who heard these things kept them in their hearts, saying, "What then will this child be?" For the Lord's hand was indeed with him.

Zechariah's Praise and Prediction
-Hill Country of Judea-

67 Then his father Zechariah was filled with the Holy Spirit and prophesied, 68 "Blessed be the Lord God of Israel, because he has come to help and has redeemed his people. 69 For he has raised up a horn of salvation for us in the house of his servant David, 70 as he spoke through the mouth of his holy prophets from long ago, 71 that we should be saved from our enemies, and from the hand of all who hate us. 72 He has done this to show mercy to our ancestors, and to remember his holy covenant – 73 the oath that he swore to our ancestor Abraham. This oath grants 74 that we, being rescued from the hand of our enemies, may serve him without fear, 75 in holiness and righteousness before him for as long as we live. 76 And you, child, will be called the prophet of the Most High. For you will go before the Lord to prepare his ways, 77 to give his people knowledge of salvation through the forgiveness of their sins. 78 Because of our God's tender mercy the dawn will break upon us from on high 79 to give light to those who sit in darkness and in the shadow of death, to guide our feet into the way of peace."

John's Growth and Early Life
Luke 1:80

80 And the child kept growing and becoming strong in spirit, and he was in the wilderness until the day he was revealed to Israel.

Jesus' Legal Lineage through Joseph
Matthew 1:1-17

1 This is the record of the genealogy of Jesus Christ, the son of David, the son of Abraham.

2 Abraham was the father of Isaac, Isaac the father of Jacob, Jacob the father of Judah and his brothers, 3 Judah the father of Perez and Zerah (by Tamar), Perez the father of Hezron, Hezron the father of Ram, 4 Ram the father of Amminadab, Amminadab the father of Nahshon, Nahshon the father of Salmon, 5 Salmon the father of Boaz (by Rahab), Boaz the father of Obed (by Ruth), Obed the father of Jesse, 6 and Jesse the father of David the king.

David was the father of Solomon (by the wife of Uriah), 7 Solomon the father of Rehoboam, Rehoboam the father of Abijah, Abijah the father of Asa, 8 Asa the father of Jehoshaphat, Jehoshaphat the father of Joram, Joram the father of Uzziah, 9

Uzziah the father of Jotham, Jotham the father of Ahaz, Ahaz the father of Hezekiah, 10 Hezekiah the father of Manasseh, Manasseh the father of Amon, Amon the father of Josiah, 11 and Josiah the father of Jeconiah and his brothers, at the time of the deportation to Babylon.

12 After the deportation to Babylon, Jeconiah became the father of Shealtiel, Shealtiel the father of Zerubbabel, 13 Zerubbabel the father of Abiud, Abiud the father of Eliakim, Eliakim the father of Azor, 14 Azor the father of Zadok, Zadok the father of Achim, Achim the father of Eliud, 15 Eliud the father of Eleazar, Eleazar the father of Matthan, Matthan the father of Jacob, 16 and Jacob the father of Joseph, the husband of Mary, by whom Jesus was born, who is called Christ.

17 So all the generations from Abraham to David are fourteen generations, and from David to the deportation to Babylon, fourteen generations, and from the deportation to Babylon to Christ, fourteen generations.

Jesus' Natural Lineage through Mary
Luke 3:23b-38

23b He was the son (as was supposed) of Joseph, the son of Heli, 24 the son of Matthat, the son of Levi, the son of Melchi, the son of Jannai, the son of Joseph, 25 the son of Mattathias, the son of Amos, the son of Nahum, the son of Esli, the son of Naggai, 26 the son of Maath, the son of Mattathias, the son of Semein, the son of Josech, the son of Joda, 27 the son of Joanan, the son of Rhesa, the son of Zerubbabel, the son of Shealtiel, the son of Neri, 28 the son of Melchi, the son of Addi, the son of Cosam, the son of Elmadam, the son of Er, 29 the son of Joshua, the son of Eliezer, the son of Jorim, the son of Matthat, the son of Levi, 30 the son of Simeon, the son of Judah, the son of Joseph, the son of Jonam, the son of Eliakim, 31 the son of Melea, the son of Menna, the son of Mattatha, the son of Nathan, the son of David, 32 the son of Jesse, the son of Obed, the son of Boaz, the son of Sala, the son of Nahshon, 33 the son of Amminadab, the son of Admin, the son of Arni, the son of Hezron, the son of Perez, the son of Judah, 34 the son of Jacob, the son of Isaac, the son of Abraham, the son of Terah, the son of Nahor, 35 the son of Serug, the son of Reu, the son of Peleg, the son of Eber, the son of Shelah, 36 the son of Cainan, the son of Arphaxad, the son of Shem, the son of Noah, the son of Lamech, 37 the son of Methuselah, the son of Enoch,

the son of Jared, the son of Mahalalel, the son of Kenan, 38 the
son of Enosh, the son of Seth, the son of Adam, the son of God.

The Prophesy of Jesus' Birth Fulfilled
-Nazareth-
Matthew 1:18-25

18 Now the birth of Jesus Christ happened this way. While his
mother Mary was engaged to Joseph, but before they came
together, she was found to be pregnant through the Holy Spirit. 19
Because Joseph, her husband to be, was a righteous man, and
because he did not want to disgrace her, he intended to divorce her
privately. 20 When he had contemplated this, an angel of the Lord
appeared to him in a dream and said, "Joseph, son of David, do
not be afraid to take Mary as your wife, because the child
conceived in her is from the Holy Spirit. 21 She will give birth to a
son and you will name him Jesus, because he will save his people
from their sins." 22 This all happened so that what was spoken by
the Lord through the prophet would be fulfilled: 23 "Look! The
virgin will conceive and bear a son, and they will call him
Emmanuel," which means "God with us." 24 When Joseph awoke
from sleep he did what the angel of the Lord told him. He took his
wife, 25 but did not have marital relations with her until she gave
birth to a son, whom he named Jesus.

The Census and the Birth of Jesus
-Bethlehem-
Luke 2:1-7

1 Now in those days a decree went out from Caesar Augustus to
register all the empire for taxes. 2 This was the first registration,
taken when Quirinius was governor of Syria. 3 Everyone went to
his own town to be registered. 4 So Joseph also went up from the
town of Nazareth in Galilee to Judea, to the city of David called
Bethlehem, because he was of the house and family line of David.
5 He went to be registered with Mary, who was promised in
marriage to him, and who was expecting a child. 6 While they
were there, the time came for her to deliver her child. 7 And she
gave birth to her firstborn son and wrapped him in strips of cloth
and laid him in a manger, because there was no place for them in
the inn.

The Shepherds and the Angels

Luke 2:8-20

8 Now there were shepherds nearby living out in the field, keeping guard over their flock at night. 9 An angel of the Lord appeared to them, and the glory of the Lord shone around them, and they were absolutely terrified. 10 But the angel said to them, "Do not be afraid! Listen carefully, for I proclaim to you good news that brings great joy to all the people: 11 Today your Savior is born in the city of David. He is Christ the Lord. 12 This will be a sign for you: You will find a baby wrapped in strips of cloth and lying in a manger." 13 Suddenly a vast, heavenly army appeared with the angel, praising God and saying, 14 "Glory to God in the highest, and on earth peace among people with whom he is pleased!"

15 When the angels left them and went back to heaven, the shepherds said to one another, "Let us go over to Bethlehem and see this thing that has taken place, that the Lord has made known to us." 16 So they hurried off and located Mary and Joseph, and found the baby lying in a manger. 17 When they saw him, they related what they had been told about this child, 18 and all who heard it were astonished at what the shepherds said. 19 But Mary treasured up all these words, pondering in her heart what they might mean. 20 So the shepherds returned, glorifying and praising God for all they had heard and seen; everything was just as they had been told.

Circumcision of Jesus
-Bethlehem-
Luke 2:21

21 At the end of eight days, when he was circumcised, he was named Jesus, the name given by the angel before he was conceived in the womb.

Jesus' Presentation at the Temple
-Jerusalem-
Luke 2:22-38

22 Now when the time came for their purification according to the law of Moses, Joseph and Mary brought Jesus up to Jerusalem to present him to the Lord 23 (just as it is written in the law of the Lord, "Every firstborn male will be set apart to the Lord"), 24 and

to offer a sacrifice according to what is specified in the law of the Lord, a pair of doves or two young pigeons.

25 Now there was a man in Jerusalem named Simeon who was righteous and devout, looking for the restoration of Israel, and the Holy Spirit was upon him. 26 It had been revealed to him by the Holy Spirit that he would not die before he had seen the Lord's Christ. 27 So Simeon, directed by the Spirit, came into the temple courts, and when the parents brought in the child Jesus to do for him what was customary according to the law, 28 Simeon took him in his arms and blessed God, saying, 29 "Now, according to your word, Sovereign Lord, permit your servant to depart in peace. 30 For my eyes have seen your salvation 31 that you have prepared in the presence of all peoples: 32 a light, for revelation to the Gentiles, and for glory to your people Israel."

33 So the child's father and mother were amazed at what was said about him. 34 Then Simeon blessed them and said to his mother Mary, "Listen carefully: This child is destined to be the cause of the falling and rising of many in Israel and to be a sign that will be rejected. 35 Indeed, as a result of him the thoughts of many hearts will be revealed – and a sword will pierce your own soul as well!"

36 There was also a prophetess, Anna the daughter of Phanuel, of the tribe of Asher. She was very old, having been married to her husband for seven years until his death. 37 She had lived as a widow since then for eighty-four years. She never left the temple, worshiping with fasting and prayer night and day. 38 At that moment, she came up to them and began to give thanks to God and to speak about the child to all who were waiting for the redemption of Jerusalem.

First Return to Nazareth
Luke 2:39

39 So when Joseph and Mary had performed everything according to the law of the Lord, they returned to Galilee, to their own town of Nazareth.

The Visit of the Magi
-Jerusalem and Nazareth-
See Note: The Visit of the Magi
Matthew 2:1-12

1 After Jesus was born in Bethlehem in Judea, in the time of King Herod, wise men from the East came to Jerusalem 2 saying, "Where is the one who is born king of the Jews? For we saw his star when it rose and have come to worship him." 3 When King Herod heard this he was alarmed, and all Jerusalem with him. 4 After assembling all the chief priests and experts in the law, he asked them where the Christ was to be born. 5 "In Bethlehem of Judea," they said, "for it is written this way by the prophet: 6 'And you, Bethlehem, in the land of Judah, are in no way least among the rulers of Judah, for out of you will come a ruler who will shepherd my people Israel.'"

7 Then Herod privately summoned the wise men and determined from them when the star had appeared. 8 He sent them to Bethlehem and said, "Go and look carefully for the child. When you find him, inform me so that I can go and worship him as well." 9 After listening to the king they left, and once again the star they saw when it rose led them until it stopped above the place where the child was. 10 When they saw the star they shouted joyfully. 11 As they came into the house and saw the child with Mary his mother, they bowed down and worshiped him. They opened their treasure boxes and gave him gifts of gold, frankincense, and myrrh. 12 After being warned in a dream not to return to Herod, they went back by another route to their own country.

The Escape to Egypt
-Nazareth and Egypt-
Matthew 2:13-18

13 After they had gone, an angel of the Lord appeared to Joseph in a dream and said, "Get up, take the child and his mother and flee to Egypt, and stay there until I tell you, for Herod is going to look for the child to kill him." 14 Then he got up, took the child and his mother during the night, and went to Egypt. 15 He stayed there until Herod died. In this way what was spoken by the Lord through the prophet was fulfilled: "I called my Son out of Egypt."

16 When Herod saw that he had been tricked by the wise men, he became enraged. He sent men to kill all the children in Bethlehem and throughout the surrounding region from the age of two and under, according to the time he had learned from the wise men. 17 Then what was spoken by Jeremiah the prophet was fulfilled: 18 "A voice was heard in Ramah, weeping and loud

wailing, Rachel weeping for her children, and she did not want to be comforted, because they were gone."

Second Return to Nazareth
-Egypt and Nazareth-
Matthew 2:19-23

19 After Herod had died, an angel of the Lord appeared in a dream to Joseph in Egypt 20 saying, "Get up, take the child and his mother, and go to the land of Israel, for those who were seeking the child's life are dead." 21 So he got up and took the child and his mother and returned to the land of Israel. 22 But when he heard that Archelaus was reigning over Judea in place of his father Herod, he was afraid to go there. After being warned in a dream, he went to the regions of Galilee. 23 He came to a town called Nazareth and lived there. Then what had been spoken by the prophets was fulfilled, that Jesus would be called a Nazarene.

Growth and Early Life of Jesus
-Nazareth-
Luke 2:40

40 And the child grew and became strong, filled with wisdom, and the favor of God was upon him.

The Boy Jesus at the Temple and First Passover
-Jerusalem-
Luke 2:41-50

41 Now Jesus' parents went to Jerusalem every year for the feast of the Passover. 42 When he was twelve years old, they went up according to custom. 43 But when the feast was over, as they were returning home, the boy Jesus stayed behind in Jerusalem. His parents did not know it, 44 but (because they assumed that he was in their group of travelers) they went a day's journey. Then they began to look for him among their relatives and acquaintances. 45 When they did not find him, they returned to Jerusalem to look for him. 46 After three days they found him in the temple courts, sitting among the teachers, listening to them and asking them questions. 47 And all who heard Jesus were astonished at his understanding and his answers. 48 When his parents saw him, they were overwhelmed. His mother said to him, "Child, why have you treated us like this? Look, your father and I have been looking for you anxiously." 49 But he replied, *"Why were you looking for me?*

Didn't you know that I must be in my Father's house?" 50 Yet his parents did not understand the remark he made to them.

Jesus Adolescence and Early Manhood
-Nazareth-
Luke 2:51-52

51 Then he went down with them and came to Nazareth, and was obedient to them. But his mother kept all these things in her heart.

52 And Jesus increased in wisdom and in stature, and in favor with God and with people.

John the Baptist Prepares the Way
-Judean Wilderness and Region around the Jordan River-
Luke 3:1-6

1 In the fifteenth year of the reign of Tiberius Caesar, when Pontius Pilate was governor of Judea, and Herod was tetrarch of Galilee, and his brother Philip was tetrarch of the region of Iturea and Trachonitis, and Lysanias was tetrarch of Abilene, 2 during the high priesthood of Annas and Caiaphas, the word of God came to John the son of Zechariah in the wilderness. 3 He went into all the region around the Jordan River, preaching a baptism of repentance for the forgiveness of sins. 4 As it is written in the book of the words of the prophet Isaiah, "The voice of one shouting in the wilderness: 'Prepare the way for the Lord, make his paths straight. 5 Every valley will be filled, and every mountain and hill will be brought low, and the crooked will be made straight, and the rough ways will be made smooth, 6 and all humanity will see the salvation of God.'"

Matthew 3:7-10

7 But when he saw many Pharisees and Sadducees coming to his baptism, he said to them, "You offspring of vipers! Who warned you to flee from the coming wrath? 8 Therefore produce fruit that proves your repentance, 9 and don't think you can say to yourselves, 'We have Abraham as our father.' For I tell you that God can raise up children for Abraham from these stones! 10 Even now the ax is laid at the root of the trees, and every tree that does not produce good fruit will be cut down and thrown into the fire.

Luke 3:10-18

10 So the crowds were asking him, "What then should we do?" 11 John answered them, "The person who has two tunics must

share with the person who has none, and the person who has food must do likewise." 12 Tax collectors also came to be baptized, and they said to him, "Teacher, what should we do?" 13 He told them, "Collect no more than you are required to." 14 Then some soldiers also asked him, "And as for us – what should we do?" He told them, "Take money from no one by violence or by false accusation, and be content with your pay."

15 While the people were filled with anticipation and they all wondered whether perhaps John could be the Christ, 16 John answered them all, "I baptize you with water, but one more powerful than I am is coming – I am not worthy to untie the strap of his sandals. He will baptize you with the Holy Spirit and fire. 17 His winnowing fork is in his hand to clean out his threshing floor and to gather the wheat into his storehouse, but the chaff he will burn up with inextinguishable fire."

18 And in this way, with many other exhortations, John proclaimed good news to the people.

The Baptism of Jesus
-Bethany beyond Jordan-
Matthew 3:13-17

13 Then Jesus came from Galilee to John to be baptized by him in the Jordan River. 14 But John tried to prevent him, saying, "I need to be baptized by you, and yet you come to me?" 15 So Jesus replied to him, *"Let it happen now, for it is right for us to fulfill all righteousness."* Then John yielded to him. 16 After Jesus was baptized, just as he was coming up out of the water, the heavens opened and he saw the Spirit of God descending like a dove and coming to rest on him. 17 And a voice from heaven said, "This is my one dear Son; in him I take great delight."

John Testifies About Jesus
-Bethany beyond Jordan-
John 1:15-18

15 John testified about him and shouted out, "This one was the one about whom I said, 'He who comes after me is greater than I am, because he existed before me.'" 16 For we have all received from his fullness one gracious gift after another. 17 For the law was given through Moses, but grace and truth came about through Jesus Christ. 18 No one has ever seen God. The only one, himself

God, who is in closest fellowship with the Father, has made God known.

The Temptation of Jesus
-Judean Wilderness-
Matthew 4:1-11

1 Then Jesus was led by the Spirit into the wilderness to be tempted by the devil. 2 After he fasted forty days and forty nights he was famished. 3 The tempter came and said to him, "If you are the Son of God, command these stones to become bread." 4 But he answered, *"It is written, 'Man does not live by bread alone, but by every word that comes from the mouth of God.'"* 5 Then the devil took him to the holy city, had him stand on the highest point of the temple, 6 and said to him, "If you are the Son of God, throw yourself down. For it is written, 'He will command his angels concerning you' and 'with their hands they will lift you up, so that you will not strike your foot against a stone.'" 7 Jesus said to him, *"Once again it is written: 'You are not to put the Lord your God to the test.'"* 8 Again, the devil took him to a very high mountain, and showed him all the kingdoms of the world and their grandeur. 9 And he said to him, "I will give you all these things if you throw yourself to the ground and worship me." 10 Then Jesus said to him, *"Go away, Satan! For it is written: 'You are to worship the Lord your God and serve only him.'"* 11 Then the devil left him, and angels came and began ministering to his needs.

John Denies Being the Christ
-Bethany beyond Jordan-
John 1:19-28

19 Now this was John's testimony when the Jewish leaders sent priests and Levites from Jerusalem to ask him, "Who are you?" 20 He confessed – he did not deny but confessed – "I am not the Christ!" 21 So they asked him, "Then who are you? Are you Elijah?" He said, "I am not!" "Are you the Prophet?" He answered, "No!" 22 Then they said to him, "Who are you? Tell us so that we can give an answer to those who sent us. What do you say about yourself?"

23 John said, "I am the voice of one shouting in the wilderness, 'Make straight the way for the Lord,' as the prophet Isaiah said." 24 (Now they had been sent from the Pharisees.) 25 So they asked

John, "Why then are you baptizing if you are not the Christ, nor Elijah, nor the Prophet?"

26 John answered them, "I baptize with water. Among you stands one whom you do not recognize, 27 who is coming after me. I am not worthy to untie the strap of his sandal!" 28 These things happened in Bethany across the Jordan River where John was baptizing.

John Identifies Jesus as the Son of God
-Bethany beyond Jordan-
John 1:29-34

29 On the next day John saw Jesus coming toward him and said, "Look, the Lamb of God who takes away the sin of the world! 30 This is the one about whom I said, 'After me comes a man who is greater than I am, because he existed before me.' 31 I did not recognize him, but I came baptizing with water so that he could be revealed to Israel."

32 Then John testified, "I saw the Spirit descending like a dove from heaven, and it remained on him. 33 And I did not recognize him, but the one who sent me to baptize with water said to me, 'The one on whom you see the Spirit descending and remaining – this is the one who baptizes with the Holy Spirit.' 34 I have both seen and testified that this man is the Chosen One of God."

Jesus' First Calling of the Disciples
-Bethany beyond Jordan and Galilee-
See Note: The Disciples of Jesus
John 1:35-42

35 Again the next day John was standing there with two of his disciples. 36 Gazing at Jesus as he walked by, he said, "Look, the Lamb of God!" 37 When John's two disciples heard him say this, they followed Jesus. 38 Jesus turned around and saw them following and said to them, *"What do you want?"* So they said to him, "Rabbi" (which is translated Teacher), "where are you staying?" 39 Jesus answered, *"Come and you will see."* So they came and saw where he was staying, and they stayed with him that day. Now it was about four o'clock in the afternoon.

40 Andrew, the brother of Simon Peter, was one of the two disciples who heard what John said and followed Jesus. 41 He first found his own brother Simon and told him, "We have found the Messiah!" (which is translated Christ). 42 Andrew brought Simon

to Jesus. Jesus looked at him and said, *"You are Simon, the son of John. You will be called Cephas"* (which is translated Peter).

Jesus' Second Calling of the Disciples
-Bethany beyond Jordan and Galilee-
See Note: The Disciples of Jesus
John 1:43-51

43 On the next day Jesus wanted to set out for Galilee. He found Philip and said to him, *"Follow me."* 44 (Now Philip was from Bethsaida, the town of Andrew and Peter.) 45 Philip found Nathanael and told him, "We have found the one Moses wrote about in the law, and the prophets also wrote about – Jesus of Nazareth, the son of Joseph." 46 Nathanael replied, "Can anything good come out of Nazareth?" Philip replied, "Come and see."

47 Jesus saw Nathanael coming toward him and exclaimed, *"Look, a true Israelite in whom there is no deceit!"* 48 Nathanael asked him, "How do you know me?" Jesus replied, *"Before Philip called you, when you were under the fig tree, I saw you."* 49 Nathanael answered him, "Rabbi, you are the Son of God; you are the king of Israel!" 50 Jesus said to him, *"Because I told you that I saw you under the fig tree, do you believe? You will see greater things than these."* 51 He continued, *"I tell all of you the solemn truth – you will see heaven opened and the angels of God ascending and descending on the Son of Man."*

First Miracle, Jesus Changes Water to Wine
-Cana of Galilee-
John 2:1-11

1 Now on the third day there was a wedding at Cana in Galilee. Jesus' mother was there, 2 and Jesus and his disciples were also invited to the wedding. 3 When the wine ran out, Jesus' mother said to him, "They have no wine left." 4 Jesus replied, *"Woman, why are you saying this to me? My time has not yet come."* 5 His mother told the servants, "Whatever he tells you, do it."

6 Now there were six stone water jars there for Jewish ceremonial washing, each holding twenty or thirty gallons. 7 Jesus told the servants, *"Fill the water jars with water."* So they filled them up to the very top. 8 Then he told them, *"Now draw some out and take it to the head steward,"* and they did. 9 When the head steward tasted the water that had been turned to wine, not knowing where it came from (though the servants who had drawn

the water knew), he called the bridegroom 10 and said to him, "Everyone serves the good wine first, and then the cheaper wine when the guests are drunk. You have kept the good wine until now!" 11 Jesus did this as the first of his miraculous signs, in Cana of Galilee. In this way he revealed his glory, and his disciples believed in him.

Jesus' Visit at Capernaum with His Mother, Brothers, and Disciples
-Capernaum-
See Note: Jesus' Brothers and Sisters
John 2:12

12 After this he went down to Capernaum with his mother and brothers and his disciples, and they stayed there a few days.

First Cleansing of the Temple at the Passover
-Jerusalem, in the Temple-
John 2:13-25

13 Now the Jewish feast of Passover was near, so Jesus went up to Jerusalem.

14 He found in the temple courts those who were selling oxen and sheep and doves, and the money changers sitting at tables. 15 So he made a whip of cords and drove them all out of the temple courts, with the sheep and the oxen. He scattered the coins of the money changers and overturned their tables. 16 To those who sold the doves he said, *"Take these things away from here! Do not make my Father's house a marketplace!"* 17 His disciples remembered that it was written, "Zeal for your house will devour me."

18 So then the Jewish leaders responded, "What sign can you show us, since you are doing these things?" 19 Jesus replied, *"Destroy this temple and in three days I will raise it up again."* 20 Then the Jewish leaders said to him, "This temple has been under construction for forty-six years, and are you going to raise it up in three days?" 21 But Jesus was speaking about the temple of his body. 22 So after he was raised from the dead, his disciples remembered that he had said this, and they believed the scripture and the saying that Jesus had spoken.

23 Now while Jesus was in Jerusalem at the feast of the Passover, many people believed in his name because they saw the miraculous signs he was doing. 24 But Jesus would not entrust

himself to them, because he knew all people. 25 He did not need anyone to testify about man, for he knew what was in man.

Jesus Teaches Nicodemus
-Jerusalem-
John 3:1-21

1 Now a certain man, a Pharisee named Nicodemus, who was a member of the Jewish ruling council, 2 came to Jesus at night and said to him, "Rabbi, we know that you are a teacher who has come from God. For no one could perform the miraculous signs that you do unless God is with him." 3 Jesus replied, *"I tell you the solemn truth, unless a person is born from above, he cannot see the kingdom of God."* 4 Nicodemus said to him, "How can a man be born when he is old? He cannot enter his mother's womb and be born a second time, can he?"

5 Jesus answered, *"I tell you the solemn truth, unless a person is born of water and spirit, he cannot enter the kingdom of God. 6 What is born of the flesh is flesh, and what is born of the Spirit is spirit. 7 Do not be amazed that I said to you, 'You must all be born from above.' 8 The wind blows wherever it will, and you hear the sound it makes, but do not know where it comes from and where it is going. So, it is with everyone who is born of the Spirit."*

9 Nicodemus replied, "How can these things be?" 10 Jesus answered, *"Are you the teacher of Israel and yet you don't understand these things? 11 I tell you the solemn truth, we speak about what we know and testify about what we have seen, but you people do not accept our testimony. 12 If I have told you people about earthly things and you don't believe, how will you believe if I tell you about heavenly things? 13 No one has ascended into heaven except the one who descended from heaven – the Son of Man. 14 Just as Moses lifted up the serpent in the wilderness, so must the Son of Man be lifted up, 15 so that everyone who believes in him may have eternal life."*

16 *"For this is the way God loved the world: He gave his one and only Son, so that everyone who believes in him will not perish but have eternal life. 17 For God did not send his Son into the world to condemn the world, but that the world should be saved through him. 18 The one who believes in him is not condemned. The one who does not believe has been condemned already, because he has not believed in the name of the one and only Son of God. 19 Now this is the basis for judging: that the light has come*

into the world and people loved the darkness rather than the light, because their deeds were evil. 20 For everyone who does evil deeds hates the light and does not come to the light, so that their deeds will not be exposed. 21 But the one who practices the truth comes to the light, so that it may be plainly evident that his deeds have been done in God."

John the Baptist's Testimony about Jesus
-Aenon near Salim-
John 3:22-36 to John 4:1-2

22 After this, Jesus and his disciples came into Judean territory, and there he spent time with them and was baptizing. 23 John was also baptizing at Aenon near Salim, because water was plentiful there, and people were coming to him and being baptized. 24 (For John had not yet been thrown into prison.)

25 Now a dispute came about between some of John's disciples and a certain Jew concerning ceremonial washing. 26 So they came to John and said to him, "Rabbi, the one who was with you on the other side of the Jordan River, about whom you testified – see, he is baptizing, and everyone is flocking to him!"

27 John replied, "No one can receive anything unless it has been given to him from heaven. 28 You yourselves can testify that I said, 'I am not the Christ,' but rather, 'I have been sent before him.' 29 The one who has the bride is the bridegroom. The friend of the bridegroom, who stands by and listens for him, rejoices greatly when he hears the bridegroom's voice. This then is my joy, and it is complete. 30 He must become more important while I become less important."

31 The one who comes from above is superior to all. The one who is from the earth belongs to the earth and speaks about earthly things. The one who comes from heaven is superior to all. 32 He testifies about what he has seen and heard, but no one accepts his testimony. 33 The one who has accepted his testimony has confirmed clearly that God is truthful. 34 For the one whom God has sent speaks the words of God, for he does not give the Spirit sparingly. 35 The Father loves the Son and has placed all things under his authority. 36 The one who believes in the Son has eternal life. The one who rejects the Son will not see life, but God's wrath remains on him.

4:1 Now when Jesus knew that the Pharisees had heard that he was winning and baptizing more disciples than John 2 (although Jesus himself was not baptizing, but his disciples were).

John the Baptist Put Into Prison
-Machaerus-
Luke 3:19-20

19 But when John rebuked Herod the tetrarch because of Herodias, his brother's wife, and because of all the evil deeds that he had done, 20 Herod added this to them all: He locked up John in prison.

Matthew 4:12

12 Now when Jesus heard that John had been imprisoned, he went into Galilee.

Jesus Talks to a Samaritan Woman
-Sychar in Samaria-
John 4:4-26

4 But he had to pass through Samaria. 5 Now he came to a Samaritan town called Sychar, near the plot of land that Jacob had given to his son Joseph. 6 Jacob's well was there, so Jesus, since he was tired from the journey, sat right down beside the well. It was about noon.

7 A Samaritan woman came to draw water. Jesus said to her, *"Give me some water to drink."* 8 (For his disciples had gone off into the town to buy supplies.) 9 So the Samaritan woman said to him, "How can you – a Jew – ask me, a Samaritan woman, for water to drink?" (For Jews use nothing in common with Samaritans.)

10 Jesus answered her, *"If you had known the gift of God and who it is who said to you, 'Give me some water to drink,' you would have asked him, and he would have given you living water."* 11 "Sir," the woman said to him, "you have no bucket and the well is deep; where then do you get this living water? 12 Surely you're not greater than our ancestor Jacob, are you? For he gave us this well and drank from it himself, along with his sons and his livestock."

13 Jesus replied, *"Everyone who drinks some of this water will be thirsty again. 14 But whoever drinks some of the water that I will give him will never be thirsty again, but the water that I will give him will become in him a fountain of water springing up to*

eternal life." 15 The woman said to him, "Sir, give me this water, so that I will not be thirsty or have to come here to draw water." 16 He said to her, *"Go call your husband and come back here."* 17 The woman replied, "I have no husband." Jesus said to her, *"Right you are when you said, 'I have no husband,' 18 for you have had five husbands, and the man you are living with now is not your husband. This you said truthfully!"*

19 The woman said to him, "Sir, I see that you are a prophet. 20 Our fathers worshiped on this mountain, and you people say that the place where people must worship is in Jerusalem." 21 Jesus said to her, *"Believe me, woman, a time is coming when you will worship the Father neither on this mountain nor in Jerusalem. 22 You people worship what you do not know. We worship what we know, because salvation is from the Jews. 23 But a time is coming – and now is here – when the true worshipers will worship the Father in spirit and truth, for the Father seeks such people to be his worshipers. 24 God is spirit, and the people who worship him must worship in spirit and truth."* 25 The woman said to him, "I know that Messiah is coming" (the one called Christ); "whenever he comes, he will tell us everything." 26 Jesus said to her, *"I, the one speaking to you, am he."*

The Disciples Rejoin Jesus
-Sychar in Samaria-
John 4:27-38

27 Now at that very moment his disciples came back. They were shocked because he was speaking with a woman. However, no one said, "What do you want?" or "Why are you speaking with her?" 28 Then the woman left her water jar, went off into the town and said to the people, 29 "Come, see a man who told me everything I ever did. Surely he can't be the Messiah, can he?" 30 So they left the town and began coming to him.

31 Meanwhile the disciples were urging him, "Rabbi, eat something." 32 But he said to them, *"I have food to eat that you know nothing about."* 33 So the disciples began to say to one another, "No one brought him anything to eat, did they?" 34 Jesus said to them, *"My food is to do the will of the one who sent me and to complete his work. 35 Don't you say, 'There are four more months and then comes the harvest?' I tell you, look up and see that the fields are already white for harvest! 36 The one who reaps receives pay and gathers fruit for eternal life, so that the one who*

sows and the one who reaps can rejoice together. 37 For in this instance the saying is true, 'One sows and another reaps.' 38 I sent you to reap what you did not work for; others have labored and you have entered into their labor."

Many Samaritans Believe
-Sychar in Samaria-
John 4:39-42

39 Now many Samaritans from that town believed in him because of the report of the woman who testified, "He told me everything I ever did." 40 So when the Samaritans came to him, they began asking him to stay with them. He stayed there two days, 41 and because of his word many more believed. 42 They said to the woman, "No longer do we believe because of your words, for we have heard for ourselves, and we know that this one really is the Savior of the world."

Jesus Returns to Galilee
John 4:43-45

43 After the two days he departed from there to Galilee. 44 (For Jesus himself had testified that a prophet has no honor in his own country.) 45 So when he came to Galilee, the Galileans welcomed him because they had seen all the things he had done in Jerusalem at the feast (for they themselves had gone to the feast).

Jesus Heals the Official's Son while at Cana in Galilee
-Cana of Galilee-
John 4:46-54

46 Now he came again to Cana in Galilee where he had made the water wine. In Capernaum there was a certain royal official whose son was sick. 47 When he heard that Jesus had come back from Judea to Galilee, he went to him and begged him to come down and heal his son, who was about to die. 48 So Jesus said to him, *"Unless you people see signs and wonders you will never believe!"* 49 "Sir," the official said to him, "come down before my child dies." 50 Jesus told him, *"Go home; your son will live."* The man believed the word that Jesus spoke to him, and set off for home.

51 While he was on his way down, his slaves met him and told him that his son was going to live. 52 So he asked them the time when his condition began to improve, and they told him,

"Yesterday at one o'clock in the afternoon the fever left him." 53 Then the father realized that it was the very time Jesus had said to him, "Your son will live," and he himself believed along with his entire household. 54 Jesus did this as his second miraculous sign when he returned from Judea to Galilee.

The Healing at the Pool
-Jerusalem-
See Note: Empty
John 5:1-15

1 After this there was a Jewish feast, and Jesus went up to Jerusalem. 2 Now there is in Jerusalem by the Sheep Gate a pool called Bethzatha in Aramaic, which has five covered walkways. 3 A great number of sick, blind, lame, and paralyzed people were lying in these walkways. 4 [[EMPTY]] 5 Now a man was there who had been disabled for thirty-eight years. 6 When Jesus saw him lying there and when he realized that the man had been disabled a long time already, he said to him, *"Do you want to become well?"* 7 The sick man answered him, "Sir, I have no one to put me into the pool when the water is stirred up. While I am trying to get into the water, someone else goes down there before me." 8 Jesus said to him, *"Stand up! Pick up your mat and walk."* 9 Immediately the man was healed, and he picked up his mat and started walking. (Now that day was a Sabbath.)

10 So the Jewish leaders said to the man who had been healed, "It is the Sabbath, and you are not permitted to carry your mat." 11 But he answered them, "The man who made me well said to me, *'Pick up your mat and walk.'*" 12 They asked him, "Who is the man who said to you, 'Pick up your mat and walk'?" 13 But the man who had been healed did not know who it was, for Jesus had slipped out, since there was a crowd in that place.

14 After this Jesus found him at the temple and said to him, *"Look, you have become well. Don't sin any more, lest anything worse happen to you."* 15 The man went away and informed the Jewish leaders that Jesus was the one who had made him well.

Jews Look to Kill Jesus
-Jerusalem-
John 5:16-18

16 Now because Jesus was doing these things on the Sabbath, the Jewish leaders began persecuting him. 17 So he told them,

"My Father is working until now, and I too am working." 18 For this reason the Jewish leaders were trying even harder to kill him, because not only was he breaking the Sabbath, but he was also calling God his own Father, thus making himself equal with God.

Life through the Son
-Jerusalem-
John 5:19-47

19 So Jesus answered them, *"I tell you the solemn truth, the Son can do nothing on his own initiative, but only what he sees the Father doing. For whatever the Father does, the Son does likewise. 20 For the Father loves the Son and shows him everything he does, and will show him greater deeds than these, so that you will be amazed. 21 For just as the Father raises the dead and gives them life, so also the Son gives life to whomever he wishes. 22 Furthermore, the Father does not judge anyone, but has assigned all judgment to the Son, 23 so that all people will honor the Son just as they honor the Father. The one who does not honor the Son does not honor the Father who sent him."*

24 *"I tell you the solemn truth, the one who hears my message and believes the one who sent me has eternal life and will not be condemned, but has crossed over from death to life. 25 I tell you the solemn truth, a time is coming – and is now here – when the dead will hear the voice of the Son of God, and those who hear will live. 26 For just as the Father has life in himself, thus he has granted the Son to have life in himself, 27 and he has granted the Son authority to execute judgment, because he is the Son of Man."*

28 *"Do not be amazed at this, because a time is coming when all who are in the tombs will hear his voice 29 and will come out – the ones who have done what is good to the resurrection resulting in life, and the ones who have done what is evil to the resurrection resulting in condemnation. 30 I can do nothing on my own initiative. Just as I hear, I judge, and my judgment is just, because I do not seek my own will, but the will of the one who sent me."*

31 *"If I testify about myself, my testimony is not true. 32 There is another who testifies about me, and I know the testimony he testifies about me is true."* 33 *"You have sent to John, and he has testified to the truth. 34 (I do not accept human testimony, but I say this so that you may be saved.) 35 He was a lamp that was burning and shining, and you wanted to rejoice greatly for a short time in his light."*

36 *"But I have a testimony greater than that from John. For the deeds that the Father has assigned me to complete – the deeds I am now doing – testify about me that the Father has sent me. 37 And the Father who sent me has himself testified about me. You people have never heard his voice nor seen his form at any time, 38 nor do you have his word residing in you, because you do not believe the one whom he sent. 39 You study the scriptures thoroughly because you think in them you possess eternal life, and it is these same scriptures that testify about me, 40 but you are not willing to come to me so that you may have life."*

41 *"I do not accept praise from people, 42 but I know you, that you do not have the love of God within you. 43 I have come in my Father's name, and you do not accept me. If someone else comes in his own name, you will accept him. 44 How can you believe, if you accept praise from one another and don't seek the praise that comes from the only God?"*

45 *"Do not suppose that I will accuse you before the Father. The one who accuses you is Moses, in whom you have placed your hope. 46 If you believed Moses, you would believe me, because he wrote about me. 47 But if you do not believe what Moses wrote, how will you believe my words?"*

Jesus Returns to Nazareth
-Nazareth-
Luke 4:14-30

14 Then Jesus, in the power of the Spirit, returned to Galilee, and news about him spread throughout the surrounding countryside. 15 He began to teach in their synagogues and was praised by all.

16 Now Jesus came to Nazareth, where he had been brought up, and went into the synagogue on the Sabbath day, as was his custom. He stood up to read, 17 and the scroll of the prophet Isaiah was given to him. He unrolled the scroll and found the place where it was written, 18 *"The Spirit of the Lord is upon me, because he has anointed me to proclaim good news to the poor. He has sent me to proclaim release to the captives and the regaining of sight to the blind, to set free those who are oppressed, 19 to proclaim the year of the Lord's favor."*

20 Then he rolled up the scroll, gave it back to the attendant, and sat down. The eyes of everyone in the synagogue were fixed on him. 21 Then he began to tell them, *"Today this scripture has*

been fulfilled even as you heard it being read." 22 All were speaking well of him, and were amazed at the gracious words coming out of his mouth. They said, "Isn't this Joseph's son?" 23 Jesus said to them, *"No doubt you will quote to me the proverb, 'Physician, heal yourself!' and say, 'What we have heard that you did in Capernaum, do here in your hometown too.'"* 24 And he added, *"I tell you the truth, no prophet is acceptable in his hometown. 25 But in truth I tell you, there were many widows in Israel in Elijah's days, when the sky was shut up three and a half years, and there was a great famine over all the land. 26 Yet Elijah was sent to none of them, but only to a woman who was a widow at Zarephath in Sidon. 27 And there were many lepers in Israel in the time of the prophet Elisha, yet none of them was cleansed except Naaman the Syrian."* 28 When they heard this, all the people in the synagogue were filled with rage. 29 They got up, forced him out of the town, and brought him to the brow of the hill on which their town was built, so that they could throw him down the cliff. 30 But he passed through the crowd and went on his way.

Jesus Leaves Nazareth and Goes to Capernaum
-Capernaum-
Matthew 4:13-17

13 While in Galilee, he moved from Nazareth to make his home in Capernaum by the sea, in the region of Zebulun and Naphtali, 14 so that what was spoken by Isaiah the prophet would be fulfilled:

15 "Land of Zebulun and land of Naphtali, the way by the sea, beyond the Jordan, Galilee of the Gentiles – 16 the people who sit in darkness have seen a great light, and on those who sit in the region and shadow of death a light has dawned."

17 From that time Jesus began to preach this message: *"Repent, for the kingdom of heaven is near."*

Jesus' Third Calling of the Disciples
-By the Sea of Galilee, near Capernaum-
See Note: The Disciples of Jesus
Matthew 4:18-22

18 As he was walking by the Sea of Galilee he saw two brothers, Simon (called Peter) and Andrew his brother, casting a net into the sea (for they were fishermen). 19 He said to them, *"Follow me, and I will turn you into fishers of people."* 20 They left their nets

immediately and followed him. 21 Going on from there he saw two other brothers, James the son of Zebedee and John his brother, in a boat with Zebedee their father, mending their nets. Then he called them. 22 They immediately left the boat and their father and followed him.

Jesus Drives out an Evil Spirit
-Capernaum-
Luke 4:31-37

31 So he went down to Capernaum, a town in Galilee, and on the Sabbath he began to teach the people. 32 They were amazed at his teaching, because he spoke with authority.

33 Now in the synagogue there was a man who had the spirit of an unclean demon, and he cried out with a loud voice, 34 "Ha! Leave us alone, Jesus the Nazarene! Have you come to destroy us? I know who you are – the Holy One of God." 35 But Jesus rebuked him: *"Silence! Come out of him!"* Then, after the demon threw the man down in their midst, he came out of him without hurting him. 36 They were all amazed and began to say to one another, "What's happening here? For with authority and power he commands the unclean spirits, and they come out!" 37 So the news about him spread into all areas of the region.

Jesus Heals Peter's Mother-in Law
-Capernaum-
Luke 4: 38-39

38 After Jesus left the synagogue, he entered Simon's house. Now Simon's mother-in-law was suffering from a high fever, and they asked Jesus to help her. 39 So he stood over her, commanded the fever, and it left her. Immediately she got up and began to serve them.

Jesus Heals Many Others
-Capernaum-
Luke 4:40-41

40 As the sun was setting, all those who had any relatives sick with various diseases brought them to Jesus. He placed his hands on every one of them and healed them. 41 Demons also came out of many, crying out, "You are the Son of God!" But he rebuked them, and would not allow them to speak, because they knew that he was the Christ.

Jesus Prays in a Solitary Place
-Capernaum-
Mark 1:35-38

35 Then Jesus got up early in the morning when it was still very dark, departed, and went out to a deserted place, and there he spent time in prayer. 36 Simon and his companions searched for him. 37 When they found him, they said, "Everyone is looking for you." 38 He replied, *"Let us go elsewhere, into the surrounding villages, so that I can preach there too. For that is what I came out here to do."*

Tour of Galilee, Jesus Heals the Sick
-Galilee-
Matthew 4:23-25

23 Jesus went throughout all of Galilee, teaching in their synagogues, preaching the gospel of the kingdom, and healing all kinds of disease and sickness among the people. 24 So a report about him spread throughout Syria. People brought to him all who suffered with various illnesses and afflictions, those who had seizures, paralytics, and those possessed by demons, and he healed them. 25 And large crowds followed him from Galilee, the Decapolis, Jerusalem, Judea, and beyond the Jordan River.

Jesus' Forth Calling of the Disciples
-By the Sea of Galilee also called the Lake of Gennesaret-
See Note: The Disciples of Jesus
Luke 5:1-11

1 Now Jesus was standing by the Lake of Gennesaret, and the crowd was pressing around him to hear the word of God. 2 He saw two boats by the lake, but the fishermen had gotten out of them and were washing their nets. 3 He got into one of the boats, which was Simon's, and asked him to put out a little way from the shore. Then Jesus sat down and taught the crowds from the boat. 4 When he had finished speaking, he said to Simon, *"Put out into the deep water and lower your nets for a catch."* 5 Simon answered, "Master, we worked hard all night and caught nothing! But at your word I will lower the nets." 6 When they had done this, they caught so many fish that their nets started to tear. 7 So they motioned to their partners in the other boat to come and help them. And they came and filled both boats, so that they were about to

sink. 8 But when Simon Peter saw it, he fell down at Jesus' knees, saying, "Go away from me, Lord, for I am a sinful man!" 9 For Peter and all who were with him were astonished at the catch of fish that they had taken, 10 and so were James and John, Zebedee's sons, who were Simon's business partners. Then Jesus said to Simon, *Do not be afraid; from now on you will be catching people.*" 11 So when they had brought their boats to shore, they left everything and followed him.

First Sermon on the Mount
-Near Capernaum-
Matthew 5:1-2

1 When he saw the crowds, he went up the mountain. After he sat down his disciples came to him. 2 Then he began to teach them by saying:

The Beatitudes
Matthew 5:3-12

3 "Blessed are the poor in spirit, for the kingdom of heaven belongs to them. 4 "Blessed are those who mourn, for they will be comforted. 5 "Blessed are the meek, for they will inherit the earth. 6 "Blessed are those who hunger and thirst for righteousness, for they will be satisfied. 7 "Blessed are the merciful, for they will be shown mercy. 8 "Blessed are the pure in heart, for they will see God. 9 "Blessed are the peacemakers, for they will be called the children of God. 10 "Blessed are those who are persecuted for righteousness, for the kingdom of heaven belongs to them. 11 "Blessed are you when people insult you and persecute you and say all kinds of evil things about you falsely on account of me. 12 Rejoice and be glad because your reward is great in heaven, for they persecuted the prophets before you in the same way."

Salt and Light
Matthew 5:13-16

13 "You are the salt of the earth. But if salt loses its flavor, how can it be made salty again? It is no longer good for anything except to be thrown out and trampled on by people. 14 You are the light of the world. A city located on a hill cannot be hidden. 15 People do not light a lamp and put it under a basket but on a lampstand, and it gives light to all in the house. 16 In the same way, let your light shine before people, so that they can see your good deeds and give honor to your Father in heaven."

The Fulfillment of the Law

Matthew 5:17-20

17 "Do not think that I have come to abolish the law or the prophets. I have not come to abolish these things but to fulfill them. 18 I tell you the truth, until heaven and earth pass away not the smallest letter or stroke of a letter will pass from the law until everything takes place. 19 So anyone who breaks one of the least of these commands and teaches others to do so will be called least in the kingdom of heaven, but whoever obeys them and teaches others to do so will be called great in the kingdom of heaven. 20 For I tell you, unless your righteousness goes beyond that of the experts in the law and the Pharisees, you will never enter the kingdom of heaven."

Murder
Matthew 5:21-26

21 "You have heard that it was said to an older generation, 'Do not murder' and 'whoever murders will be subjected to judgment.' 22 But I say to you that anyone who is angry with a brother will be subjected to judgment. And whoever insults a brother will be brought before the council, and whoever says 'Fool' will be sent to fiery hell." 23 "So then, if you bring your gift to the altar and there remember that your brother has something against you, 24 leave your gift there in front of the altar. First go and be reconciled to your brother and then come and present your gift." 25 "Reach agreement quickly with your accuser while on the way to court, or he may hand you over to the judge, and the judge hand you over to the warden, and you will be thrown into prison. 26 I tell you the truth; you will never get out of there until you have paid the last penny!"

Adultery
Matthew 5:27-30

27 "You have heard that it was said, 'Do not commit adultery.' 28 But I say to you that whoever looks at a woman to desire her has already committed adultery with her in his heart. 29 If your right eye causes you to sin, tear it out and throw it away! It is better to lose one of your members than to have your whole body thrown into hell. 30 If your right hand causes you to sin, cut it off and throw it away! It is better to lose one of your members than to have your whole body go into hell."

Divorce
Matthew 5:31-32

31 "It was said, 'Whoever divorces his wife must give her a legal document.' 32 But I say to you that everyone who divorces his wife, except for immorality, makes her commit adultery, and whoever marries a divorced woman commits adultery."

Oaths

Matthew 5:33-37

33 "Again, you have heard that it was said to an older generation, 'Do not break an oath, but fulfill your vows to the Lord.' 34 But I say to you, do not take oaths at all – not by heaven, because it is the throne of God, 35 not by earth, because it is his footstool, and not by Jerusalem, because it is the city of the great King. 36 Do not take an oath by your head, because you are not able to make one hair white or black. 37 Let your word be 'Yes, yes' or 'No, no.' More than this is from the evil one."

An Eye for an Eye

Matthew 5:38-42

38 "You have heard that it was said, 'An eye for an eye and a tooth for a tooth.' 39 But I say to you, do not resist the evildoer. But whoever strikes you on the right cheek, turn the other to him as well. 40 And if someone wants to sue you and to take your tunic, give him your coat also. 41 And if anyone forces you to go one mile, go with him two. 42 Give to the one who asks you, and do not reject the one who wants to borrow from you."

Love for Enemies

Matthew 5:43-48

43 "You have heard that it was said, 'Love your neighbor' and 'hate your enemy.' 44 But I say to you, love your enemy and pray for those who persecute you, 45 so that you may be like your Father in heaven, since he causes the sun to rise on the evil and the good, and sends rain on the righteous and the unrighteous. 46 For if you love those who love you, what reward do you have? Even the tax collectors do the same, don't they? 47 And if you only greet your brothers, what more do you do? Even the Gentiles do the same, don't they? 48 So then, be perfect, as your heavenly Father is perfect."

Giving to the Needy

Matthew 6:1-4

1 "Be careful not to display your righteousness merely to be seen by people. Otherwise you have no reward with your Father in heaven." 2 "So whenever you do charitable giving, do not blow a trumpet before you, as the hypocrites do in synagogues and on streets so that people will praise them. I tell you the truth, they have their reward. 3 But when you do your giving, do not let your left hand know what your right hand is doing, 4 so that your gift may be in secret. And your Father, who sees in secret, will reward you."

Prayer
Matthew 6:5-15

5 "Whenever you pray, do not be like the hypocrites, because they love to pray while standing in synagogues and on street corners so that people can see them. Truly I say to you, they have their reward. 6 But whenever you pray, go into your room, close the door, and pray to your Father in secret. And your Father, who sees in secret, will reward you. 7 When you pray, do not babble repetitiously like the Gentiles, because they think that by their many words they will be heard. 8 Do not be like them, for your Father knows what you need before you ask him." 9 "So pray this way: Our Father in heaven, may your name be honored, 10 may your kingdom come, may your will be done on earth as it is in heaven. 11 Give us today our daily bread, 12 and forgive us our debts, as we ourselves have forgiven our debtors. 13 And do not lead us into temptation, but deliver us from the evil one.

14 "For if you forgive others their sins, your heavenly Father will also forgive you. 15 But if you do not forgive others, your Father will not forgive you your sins."

Fasting
Matthew 6:16-18

16 "When you fast, do not look sullen like the hypocrites, for they make their faces unattractive so that people will see them fasting. I tell you the truth, they have their reward. 17 When you fast, put oil on your head and wash your face, 18 so that it will not be obvious to others when you are fasting, but only to your Father who is in secret. And your Father, who sees in secret, will reward you."

Treasures in Heaven
Matthew 6:19-21

19 "Do not accumulate for yourselves treasures on earth, where moth and rust destroy and where thieves break in and steal. 20 But accumulate for yourselves treasures in heaven, where moth and rust do not destroy, and thieves do not break in and steal. 21 For where your treasure is, there your heart will be also."

The Lamp of the Body

Luke 11:33-36

33 "No one after lighting a lamp puts it in a hidden place or under a basket, but on a lampstand, so that those who come in can see the light. 34 Your eye is the lamp of your body. When your eye is healthy, your whole body is full of light, but when it is diseased, your body is full of darkness. 35 Therefore see to it that the light in you is not darkness. 36 If then your whole body is full of light, with no part in the dark, it will be as full of light as when the light of a lamp shines on you."

Serving Two Masters
Matthew 6:24

24 "No one can serve two masters, for either he will hate the one and love the other, or he will be devoted to the one and despise the other. You cannot serve God and money."

Do Not Worry
Matthew 6:25-34

25 "Therefore I tell you, do not worry about your life, what you will eat or drink, or about your body, what you will wear. Isn't there more to life than food and more to the body than clothing? 26 Look at the birds in the sky: They do not sow, or reap, or gather into barns, yet your heavenly Father feeds them. Aren't you more valuable than they are? 27 And which of you by worrying can add even one hour to his life?" 28 "Why do you worry about clothing? Think about how the flowers of the field grow; they do not work or spin. 29 Yet I tell you that not even Solomon in all his glory was clothed like one of these! 30 And if this is how God clothes the wild grass, which is here today and tomorrow is tossed into the fire to heat the oven, won't he clothe you even more, you people of little faith? 31 So then, don't worry saying, 'What will we eat?' or 'What will we drink?' or 'What will we wear?' 32 For the unconverted pursue these things, and your heavenly Father knows that you need them. 33 But above all pursue his kingdom and righteousness, and all these things will be given to you as well. 34 So then, do not worry about tomorrow, for tomorrow will worry about itself. Today has enough trouble of its own."

Luke 12:32-34

32 "Do not be afraid, little flock, for your Father is well pleased to give you the kingdom. 33 Sell your possessions and give to the poor. Provide yourselves purses that do not wear out – a treasure in heaven that never decreases, where no thief approaches and no moth destroys. 34 For where your treasure is, there your heart will be also."

Judging Others
Matthew 7:1-6

1 "Do not judge so that you will not be judged. 2 For by the standard you judge you will be judged, and the measure you use will be the measure you receive." 3 "Why do you see the speck in your brother's eye, but fail to see the beam of wood in your own? 4 Or how can you say to your brother, 'Let me remove the speck from your eye,' while there is a beam in your own? 5 You hypocrite! First remove the beam from your own eye, and then you can see clearly to remove the speck from your brother's eye." 6 "Do not give what is holy to dogs or throw your pearls before pigs; otherwise they will trample them under their feet and turn around and tear you to pieces."

Ask, Seek, Knock
Matthew 7:7-12

7 "Ask and it will be given to you; seek and you will find; knock and the door will be opened for you. 8 For everyone who asks receives, and the one who seeks finds, and to the one who knocks, the door will be opened." 9 "Is there anyone among you who, if his son asks for bread, will give him a stone? 10 Or if he asks for a fish, will give him a snake? 11 If you then, although you are evil, know how to give good gifts to your children, how much more will your Father in heaven give good gifts to those who ask him! 12 In everything, treat others as you would want them to treat you, for this fulfills the law and the prophets."

The Narrow and Wide Gates
Matthew 7:13-14

13 "Enter through the narrow gate, because the gate is wide and the way is spacious that leads to destruction, and there are many who enter through it. 14 How narrow is the gate and difficult the way that leads to life, and there are few who find it!"

A Tree and Its Fruit
Matthew 7:15-23

15 "Watch out for false prophets, who come to you in sheep's clothing but inwardly are voracious wolves. 16 You will recognize them by their fruit. Grapes are not gathered from thorns or figs from thistles, are they? 17 In the same way, every good tree bears good fruit, but the bad tree bears bad fruit." 18 "A good tree is not able to bear bad fruit, nor a bad tree to bear good fruit. 19 Every tree that does not bear good fruit is cut down and thrown into the fire. 20 So then, you will recognize them by their fruit."

21 "Not everyone who says to me, 'Lord, Lord,' will enter into the kingdom of heaven – only the one who does the will of my Father in heaven. 22 On that day, many will say to me, 'Lord, Lord, didn't we prophesy in your name, and cast out demons in your name, and do many powerful deeds in your name?' 23 Then I will declare to them, 'I never knew you. Go away from me, you lawbreakers!'"

The Wise and Foolish Builders
Matthew 7:24-29

24 "Everyone who hears these words of mine and does them is like a wise man who built his house on rock. 25 The rain fell, the flood came, and the winds beat against that house, but it did not collapse because its foundation had been laid on rock. 26 Everyone who hears these words of mine and does not do them is like a foolish man who built his house on sand. 27 The rain fell, the flood came, and the winds beat against that house, and it collapsed – it was utterly destroyed!"

28 When Jesus finished saying these things, the crowds were amazed by his teaching, 29 because he taught them like one who had authority, not like their experts in the law.

Jesus Heals a Man with Leprosy
-One of the Cities by the Sea of Galilee-
Luke 5:12-16

12 While Jesus was in one of the towns, a man came to him who was covered with leprosy. When he saw Jesus, he bowed down with his face to the ground and begged him, "Lord, if you are willing, you can make me clean." 13 So he stretched out his hand and touched him, saying, "I am willing. Be clean!" And immediately the leprosy left him. 14 Then he ordered the man to tell no one, but commanded him, "Don't tell anyone, but go and show yourself to a priest, and bring the offering for your cleansing, as Moses commanded, as a testimony to them." 15 But the news about him spread even more, and large crowds were gathering together to hear him and to be healed of their illnesses. 16 Yet Jesus himself frequently withdrew to the wilderness and prayed.

Forgiving and Healing of a Paralytic

-Capernaum-
Luke 5:17-26

17 Now on one of those days, while he was teaching, there were
Pharisees and teachers of the law sitting nearby (who had come
from every village of Galilee and Judea and from Jerusalem), and
the power of the Lord was with him to heal. 18 Just then some
men showed up, carrying a paralyzed man on a stretcher. They
were trying to bring him in and place him before Jesus. 19 But
since they found no way to carry him in because of the crowd,
they went up on the roof and let him down on the stretcher through
the roof tiles right in front of Jesus. 20 When Jesus saw their faith
he said, *"Friend, your sins are forgiven."* 21 Then the experts in
the law and the Pharisees began to think to themselves, "Who is
this man who is uttering blasphemies? Who can forgive sins but
God alone?" 22 When Jesus perceived their hostile thoughts, he
said to them, *"Why are you raising objections within yourselves?
23 Which is easier, to say, 'Your sins are forgiven,' or to say,
'Stand up and walk'? 24 But so that you may know that the Son of
Man has authority on earth to forgive sins"* – he said to the
paralyzed man – *"I tell you, stand up, take your stretcher and go
home."* 25 Immediately he stood up before them, picked up the
stretcher he had been lying on, and went home, glorifying God. 26
Then astonishment seized them all, and they glorified God. They
were filled with awe, saying, "We have seen incredible things
today."

The Calling of Matthew
-Capernaum-
Mark 2:13-14
See Note: The Disciples of Jesus

13 Jesus went out again by the sea. The whole crowd came to him,
and he taught them. 14 As he went along, he saw Levi, the son of
Alphaeus, sitting at the tax booth. *"Follow me,"* he said to him.
And he got up and followed him.

Banquet at Matthew's House
-Capernaum-
Luke 5:29-32

29 Then Levi gave a great banquet in his house for Jesus, and
there was a large crowd of tax collectors and others sitting at the
table with them. 30 But the Pharisees and their experts in the law

complained to his disciples, saying, "Why do you eat and drink with tax collectors and sinners?" 31 Jesus answered them, *"Those who are well don't need a physician, but those who are sick do. 32 I have not come to call the righteous, but sinners to repentance."*

Jesus Questioned About Fasting
-Capernaum-
Luke 5:33-39

33 Then they said to him, "John's disciples frequently fast and pray, and so do the disciples of the Pharisees, but yours continue to eat and drink." 34 So Jesus said to them, *"You cannot make the wedding guests fast while the bridegroom is with them, can you? 35 But those days are coming, and when the bridegroom is taken from them, at that time they will fast."* 36 He also told them a parable: *"No one tears a patch from a new garment and sews it on an old garment. If he does, he will have torn the new, and the piece from the new will not match the old. 37 And no one pours new wine into old wineskins. If he does, the new wine will burst the skins and will be spilled, and the skins will be destroyed. 38 Instead new wine must be poured into new wineskins. 39 No one after drinking old wine wants the new, for he says, 'The old is good enough.'"*

Lord of the Sabbath
-Probably Galilee-
Matthew 12:1-8

1 At that time Jesus went through the grain fields on a Sabbath. His disciples were hungry, and they began to pick heads of wheat and eat them. 2 But when the Pharisees saw this they said to him, "Look, your disciples are doing what is against the law to do on the Sabbath." 3 He said to them, *"Haven't you read what David did when he and his companions were hungry – 4 how he entered the house of God and they ate the sacred bread, which was against the law for him or his companions to eat, but only for the priests? 5 Or have you not read in the law that the priests in the temple desecrate the Sabbath and yet are not guilty? 6 I tell you that something greater than the temple is here. 7 If you had known what this means: 'I want mercy and not sacrifice,' you would not have condemned the innocent. 8 For the Son of Man is lord of the Sabbath."*

Jesus Heals the Withered Hand of a Man on the Sabbath
-In a Synagogue in Galilee-
Matthew 12:9-14

9 Then Jesus left that place and entered their synagogue. 10 A man was there who had a withered hand. And they asked Jesus, "Is it lawful to heal on the Sabbath?" so that they could accuse him. 11 He said to them, *"Would not any one of you, if he had one sheep that fell into a pit on the Sabbath, take hold of it and lift it out? 12 How much more valuable is a person than a sheep! So, it is lawful to do good on the Sabbath."* 13 Then he said to the man, *"Stretch out your hand."* He stretched it out and it was restored, as healthy as the other. 14 But the Pharisees went out and plotted against him, as to how they could assassinate him.

God's Chosen Servant
-Galilee-
Matthew 12:15-21

15 Now when Jesus learned of this, he went away from there. Great crowds followed him, and he healed them all. 16 But he sternly warned them not to make him known. 17 This fulfilled what was spoken by the prophet Isaiah: 18 "Here is my servant whom I have chosen, the one I love, in whom I take great delight. I will put my Spirit on him, and he will proclaim justice to the nations. 19 He will not quarrel or cry out, nor will anyone hear his voice in the streets. 20 He will not break a bruised reed or extinguish a smoldering wick, until he brings justice to victory. 21 And in his name the Gentiles will hope."

Jesus Withdraws to the Sea of Galilee
-Galilee-
Mark 3:7-12

7 Then Jesus went away with his disciples to the sea, and a great multitude from Galilee followed him. And from Judea, 8 Jerusalem, Idumea, beyond the Jordan River, and around Tyre and Sidon a great multitude came to him when they heard about the things he had done. 9 Because of the crowd, he told his disciples to have a small boat ready for him so the crowd would not press toward him. 10 For he had healed many, so that all who were afflicted with diseases pressed toward him in order to touch him. 11 And whenever the unclean spirits saw him, they fell down

before him and cried out, "You are the Son of God." 12 But he sternly ordered them not to make him known.

Jesus Appoints the Twelve Apostles
-A mountain near the Sea of Galilee-
See Note: The Twelve Apostles
Luke 6:12-16

12 Now it was during this time that Jesus went out to the mountain to pray, and he spent all night in prayer to God. 13 When morning came, he called his disciples and chose twelve of them, whom he also named apostles: 14 Simon (whom he named Peter), and his brother Andrew; and James, John, Philip, Bartholomew, 15 Matthew, Thomas, James the son of Alphaeus, Simon who was called the Zealot, 16 Judas the son of James, and Judas Iscariot, who became a traitor.

Second Sermon on the Mount
-A mountain near the Sea of Galilee-
Luke 6:17-19

17 Then he came down with them and stood on a level place. And a large number of his disciples had gathered along with a vast multitude from all over Judea, from Jerusalem, and from the seacoast of Tyre and Sidon. They came to hear him and to be healed of their diseases, 18 and those who suffered from unclean spirits were cured. 19 The whole crowd was trying to touch him, because power was coming out from him and healing them all.

Blessings and Woes
Luke 6:20-26

20 Then he looked up at his disciples and said: *"Blessed are you who are poor, for the kingdom of God belongs to you. 21 "Blessed are you who hunger now, for you will be satisfied. "Blessed are you who weep now, for you will laugh. 22 "Blessed are you when people hate you, and when they exclude you and insult you and reject you as evil on account of the Son of Man! 23 Rejoice in that day, and jump for joy, because your reward is great in heaven. For their ancestors did the same things to the prophets. 24 "But woe to you who are rich, for you have received your comfort already." 25 "Woe to you who are well satisfied with food now, for you will be hungry." "Woe to you who laugh now, for you will mourn and weep." 26 "Woe to you when all people speak well of you, for their ancestors did the same things to the false prophets."*

Love for Enemies
Luke 6:27-36

27 "But I say to you who are listening: Love your enemies, do good to those who hate you, 28 bless those who curse you, pray for those who mistreat you. 29 To the person who strikes you on the cheek, offer the other as well, and from the person, who takes away your coat, do not withhold your tunic either. 30 Give to everyone who asks you, and do not ask for your possessions back from the person who takes them away. 31 Treat others in the same way that you would want them to treat you."

32 "If you love those who love you, what credit is that to you? For even sinners love those who love them. 33 And if you do good to those who do good to you, what credit is that to you? Even sinners do the same. 34 And if you lend to those from whom you hope to be repaid, what credit is that to you? Even sinners lend to sinners, so that they may be repaid in full. 35 But love your enemies, and do good, and lend, expecting nothing back. Then your reward will be great, and you will be sons of the Most High, because he is kind to ungrateful and evil people. 36 Be merciful, just as your Father is merciful."

Judging Others
Luke 6:37-42

37 "Do not judge, and you will not be judged; do not condemn, and you will not be condemned; forgive, and you will be forgiven. 38 Give and it will be given to you: A good measure, pressed down, shaken together, running over, will be poured into your lap. For the measure you use will be the measure you receive."

39 He also told them a parable: *"Someone who is blind cannot lead another who is blind, can he? Won't they both fall into a pit? 40 A disciple is not greater than his teacher, but everyone when fully trained will be like his teacher."* 41 *"Why do you see the speck in your brother's eye, but fail to see the beam of wood in your own? 42 How can you say to your brother, 'Brother, let me remove the speck from your eye,' while you yourself don't see the beam in your own? You hypocrite! First remove the beam from your own eye, and then you can see clearly to remove the speck from your brother's eye."*

A Tree and its Fruit
Luke 6:43-45

43 "For no good tree bears bad fruit, nor again does a bad tree bear good fruit, 44 for each tree is known by its own fruit. For figs are not gathered from thorns, nor are grapes picked from brambles. 45 The good person out of the good treasury of his heart produces good, and the evil person out of his evil treasury produces evil, for his mouth speaks from what fills his heart."

The Wise and Foolish Builders

Luke 6:46-49

46 "Why do you call me 'Lord, Lord,' and don't do what I tell you?

47 "Everyone who comes to me and listens to my words and puts them into practice – I will show you what he is like: 48 He is like a man building a house, who dug down deep, and laid the foundation on bedrock. When a flood came, the river burst against that house but could not shake it, because it had been well built. 49 But the person who hears and does not put my words into practice is like a man who built a house on the ground without a foundation. When the river burst against that house, it collapsed immediately, and was utterly destroyed!"

The Faith of the Centurion
-Capernaum-
Matthew 8:5-13

5 When he entered Capernaum, a centurion came to him asking for help: 6 "Lord, my servant is lying at home paralyzed, in terrible anguish." 7 Jesus said to him, *"I will come and heal him."* 8 But the centurion replied, "Lord, I am not worthy to have you come under my roof! Instead, just say the word and my servant will be healed. 9 For I too am a man under authority, with soldiers under me. I say to this one, 'Go!' and he goes, and to another 'Come!' and he comes, and to my slave 'Do this!' and he does it." 10 When Jesus heard this he was amazed and said to those who followed him, *"I tell you the truth, I have not found such faith in anyone in Israel! 11 I tell you, many will come from the east and west to share the banquet with Abraham, Isaac, and Jacob in the kingdom of heaven, 12 but the sons of the kingdom will be thrown out into the outer darkness, where there will be weeping and gnashing of teeth."* 13 Then Jesus said to the centurion, *"Go; just as you believed, it will be done for you."* And the servant was healed at that hour.

Jesus Raises a Widow's Son
-Nain-

11 Soon afterward Jesus went to a town called Nain, and his disciples and a large crowd went with him. 12 As he approached the town gate, a man who had died was being carried out, the only son of his mother (who was a widow), and a large crowd from the town was with her. 13 When the Lord saw her, he had compassion for her and said to her, *"Do not weep."* 14 Then he came up and touched the bier, and those who carried it stood still. He said, *"Young man, I say to you, get up!"* 15 So the dead man sat up and began to speak, and Jesus gave him back to his mother. 16 Fear seized them all, and they began to glorify God, saying, "A great prophet has appeared among us!" and "God has come to help his people!" 17 This report about Jesus circulated throughout Judea and all the surrounding country.

Jesus and John the Baptist
-Galilee-
Luke 7:18-35

18 John's disciples informed him about all these things. So John called two of his disciples 19 and sent them to Jesus to ask, "Are you the one who is to come, or should we look for another?" 20 When the men came to Jesus, they said, "John the Baptist has sent us to you to ask, 'Are you the one who is to come, or should we look for another?'" 21 At that very time Jesus cured many people of diseases, sicknesses, and evil spirits, and granted sight to many who were blind. 22 So he answered them, *"Go tell John what you have seen and heard: The blind see, the lame walk, lepers are cleansed, the deaf hear, the dead are raised, the poor have good news proclaimed to them. 23 Blessed is anyone who takes no offense at me."*

24 When John's messengers had gone, Jesus began to speak to the crowds about John: *"What did you go out into the wilderness to see? A reed shaken by the wind? 25 What did you go out to see? A man dressed in soft clothing? Look, those who wear soft clothing and live in luxury are in the royal palaces! 26 What did you go out to see? A prophet? Yes, I tell you, and more than a prophet. 27 This is the one about whom it is written, 'Look, I am sending my messenger ahead of you, who will prepare your way before you.' 28 I tell you; among those born of women no one is greater than John. Yet the one who is least in the kingdom of God is greater than he is."* 29 (Now all the people who heard this, even

the tax collectors, acknowledged God's justice, because they had been baptized with John's baptism. 30 However, the Pharisees and the experts in religious law rejected God's purpose for themselves, because they had not been baptized by John.)

31 "To what then should I compare the people of this generation, and what are they like? 32 They are like children sitting in the marketplace and calling out to one another, 'We played the flute for you, yet you did not dance; we wailed in mourning, yet you did not weep.' 33 For John the Baptist has come eating no bread and drinking no wine, and you say, 'He has a demon!' 34 The Son of Man has come eating and drinking, and you say, 'Look at him, a glutton and a drunk, a friend of tax collectors and sinners!' 35 But wisdom is vindicated by all her children."

Woe on Unrepentant Cities
-Galilee-
Matthew 11:20-30

20 Then Jesus began to criticize openly the cities in which he had done many of his miracles, because they did not repent. 21 *"Woe to you, Chorazin! Woe to you, Bethsaida! If the miracles done in you had been done in Tyre and Sidon, they would have repented long ago in sackcloth and ashes. 22 But I tell you, it will be more bearable for Tyre and Sidon on the Day of Judgment than for you! 23 And you, Capernaum, will you be exalted to heaven? No, you will be thrown down to Hades! For if the miracles done among you had been done in Sodom, it would have continued to this day. 24 But I tell you, it will be more bearable for the region of Sodom on the Day of Judgment than for you!"*

25 At that time Jesus said, *"I praise you, Father, Lord of heaven and earth, because you have hidden these things from the wise and intelligent, and have revealed them to little children. 26 Yes, Father, for this was your gracious will. 27 All things have been handed over to me by my Father. No one knows the Son except the Father, and no one knows the Father except the Son and anyone to whom the Son decides to reveal him. 28 Come to me, all you who are weary and burdened, and I will give you rest. 29 Take my yoke on you and learn from me, because I am gentle and humble in heart, and you will find rest for your souls. 30 For my yoke is easy to bear, and my load is not hard to carry."*

Jesus Anointed by a Sinful Woman
-Galilee-
See Note: Jesus Anointed
Luke 7:36-50

36 Now one of the Pharisees asked Jesus to have dinner with him, so he went into the Pharisee's house and took his place at the table. 37 Then when a woman of that town, who was a sinner, learned that Jesus was dining at the Pharisee's house, she brought an alabaster jar of perfumed oil. 38 As she stood behind him at his feet, weeping, she began to wet his feet with her tears. She wiped them with her hair, kissed them, and anointed them with the perfumed oil. 39 Now when the Pharisee who had invited him saw this, he said to himself, "If this man were a prophet, he would know who and what kind of woman this is who is touching him, that she is a sinner." 40 So Jesus answered him, *"Simon, I have something to say to you."* He replied, "Say it, Teacher." *41 "A certain creditor had two debtors; one owed him five hundred silver coins, and the other fifty. 42 When they could not pay, he canceled the debts of both. Now which of them will love him more?"* 43 Simon answered, "I suppose the one who had the bigger debt canceled." Jesus said to him, *"You have judged rightly."* 44 Then, turning toward the woman, he said to Simon, *"Do you see this woman? I entered your house. You gave me no water for my feet, but she has wet my feet with her tears and wiped them with her hair. 45 You gave me no kiss of greeting, but from the time I entered she has not stopped kissing my feet. 46 You did not anoint my head with oil, but she has anointed my feet with perfumed oil. 47 Therefore I tell you, her sins, which were many, are forgiven, thus she loved much; but the one who is forgiven little loves little."* 48 Then Jesus said to her, *"Your sins are forgiven."* 49 But those who were at the table with him began to say among themselves, "Who is this, who even forgives sins?" 50 He said to the woman, *"Your faith has saved you; go in peace."*

Jesus' Ministry and the Help of Women
-Galilee-
Luke 8:1-3

1 Sometime afterward he went on through towns and villages, preaching and proclaiming the good news of the kingdom of God. The twelve were with him, 2 and also some women who had been healed of evil spirits and disabilities: Mary (called Magdalene),

from whom seven demons had gone out, 3 and Joanna the wife of Cuza (Herod's household manager), Susanna, and many others who provided for them out of their own resources.

Jesus Heals a Demon Possessed Man
-Galilee-
Mark 3:20-21
20 Now Jesus went home, and a crowd gathered so that they were not able to eat. 21 When his family heard this they went out to restrain him, for they said, "He is out of his mind."
Matthew 12:22-23
22 Then they brought to him a demon-possessed man who was blind and mute. Jesus healed him so that he could speak and see. 23 All the crowds were amazed and said, "Could this one be the Son of David?"

Blasphemy against the Holy Spirit
-Galilee-
See Note: Blasphemy against the Holy Spirit
Matthew 12:24
24 But when the Pharisees heard this they said, "He does not cast out demons except by the power of Beelzebub, the ruler of demons!"
Luke 11:17-22
17 But Jesus, realizing their thoughts, said to them, *"Every kingdom divided against itself is destroyed, and a divided household falls. 18 So if Satan too is divided against himself, how will his kingdom stand? I ask you this because you claim that I cast out demons by Beelzebub. 19 Now if I cast out demons by Beelzebub, by whom do your sons cast them out? Therefore, they will be your judges. 20 But if I cast out demons by the finger of God, then the kingdom of God has already overtaken you. 21 When a strong man, fully armed, guards his own palace, his possessions are safe. 22 But when a stronger man attacks and conquers him, he takes away the first man's armor on which the man relied and divides up his plunder."*
Mark 3:28-30
28 "I tell you the truth; people will be forgiven for all sins, even all the blasphemies they utter. 29 But whoever blasphemes against the Holy Spirit will never be forgiven, but is guilty of an eternal sin" 30 (because they said, "He has an unclean spirit").

23 "Whoever is not with me is against me, and whoever does not gather with me scatters."

24 "When an unclean spirit goes out of a person, it passes through waterless places looking for rest but not finding any. Then it says, 'I will return to the home I left.' 25 When it returns, it finds the house swept clean and put in order. 26 Then it goes and brings seven other spirits more evil than itself, and they go in and live there, so the last state of that person is worse than the first."

27 As he said these things, a woman in the crowd spoke out to him, "Blessed is the womb that bore you and the breasts at which you nursed!" 28 But he replied, *"Blessed rather are those who hear the word of God and obey it!"*

The Sign of Jonah
-Galilee-
Matthew 12:38-42

38 Then some of the experts in the law along with some Pharisees answered him, "Teacher, we want to see a sign from you." 39 But he answered them, *"An evil and adulterous generation asks for a sign, but no sign will be given to it except the sign of the prophet Jonah. 40 For just as Jonah was in the belly of the huge fish for three days and three nights, so the Son of Man will be in the heart of the earth for three days and three nights. 41 The people of Nineveh will stand up at the judgment with this generation and condemn it, because they repented when Jonah preached to them – and now, something greater than Jonah is here! 42 The queen of the south will rise up at the judgment with this generation and condemn it, because she came from the ends of the earth to hear the Wisdom of Solomon – and now, something greater than Solomon is here!"*

Jesus' Mother and Brothers
-Galilee-
Matthew 12:46-50
See Note: Jesus' Brothers and Sisters

46 While Jesus was still speaking to the crowds, his mother and brothers came and stood outside, asking to speak to him. 47 Someone told him, "Look, your mother and your brothers are standing outside wanting to speak to you." 48 To the one who had said this, Jesus replied, *"Who is my mother and who are my*

brothers?" 49 And pointing toward his disciples he said, *"Here are my mother and my brothers! 50 For whoever does the will of my Father in heaven is my brother and sister and mother."*

Jesus Teaches in Parables
-By the Sea of Galilee-
Matthew 13:1-3a

1 On that day after Jesus went out of the house, he sat by the lake. 2 And such a large crowd gathered around him that he got into a boat to sit while the whole crowd stood on the shore. 3a He told them many things in parables, saying:

The Parable of the Sower
Matthew 13:3b-23

3b "Listen! A sower went out to sow. 4 And as he sowed, some seeds fell along the path, and the birds came and devoured them. 5 Other seeds fell on rocky ground where they did not have much soil. They sprang up quickly because the soil was not deep. 6 But when the sun came up, they were scorched, and because they did not have sufficient root, they withered. 7 Other seeds fell among the thorns, and they grew up and choked them. 8 But other seeds fell on good soil and produced grain, some a hundred times as much, some sixty, and some thirty. 9 The one who has ears had better listen!"

10 Then the disciples came to him and said, "Why do you speak to them in parables?" 11 He replied, *"You have been given the opportunity to know the secrets of the kingdom of heaven, but they have not. 12 For whoever has will be given more, and will have an abundance. But whoever does not have, even what he has will be taken from him. 13 For this reason I speak to them in parables: Although they see they do not see, and although they hear they do not hear nor do they understand. 14 And concerning them the prophecy of Isaiah is fulfilled that says: 'You will listen carefully yet will never understand; you will look closely yet will never comprehend. 15 For the heart of this people has become dull; they are hard of hearing, and they have shut their eyes, so that they would not see with their eyes and hear with their ears and understand with their hearts and turn, and I would heal them.'*

16 "But your eyes are blessed because they see, and your ears because they hear. 17 For I tell you the truth, many prophets and righteous people longed to see what you see but did not see it, and to hear what you hear but did not hear it."

18 *"So listen to the parable of the sower: 19 When anyone hears the word about the kingdom and does not understand it, the evil one comes and snatches what was sown in his heart; this is the seed sown along the path. 20 The seed sown on rocky ground is the person who hears the word and immediately receives it with joy. 21 But he has no root in himself and does not endure; when trouble or persecution comes because of the word, immediately he falls away. 22 The seed sown among thorns is the person who hears the word, but worldly cares and the seductiveness of wealth choke the word, so it produces nothing. 23 But as for the seed sown on good soil, this is the person who hears the word and understands. He bears fruit, yielding a hundred, sixty, or thirty times what was sown."*

The Parable of the Lamp on a Stand
Mark 4:21-25

21 He also said to them, *"A lamp isn't brought to be put under a basket or under a bed, is it? Isn't it to be placed on a lampstand? 22 For nothing is hidden except to be revealed, and nothing concealed except to be brought to light. 23 If anyone has ears to hear, he had better listen!"* 24 And he said to them, *"Take care about what you hear. The measure you use will be the measure you receive, and more will be added to you. 25 For whoever has will be given more, but whoever does not have, even what he has will be taken from him."*

The Parable of the Weeds
Matthew 13:24-30

24 He presented them with another parable: *"The kingdom of heaven is like a person who sowed good seed in his field. 25 But while everyone was sleeping, an enemy came and sowed darnel among the wheat and went away. 26 When the plants sprouted and produced grain, then the darnel also appeared."* 27 *"So the slaves of the landowner came and said to him, 'Sir, didn't you sow good seed in your field? Then where did the darnel come from?'"* 28 *"He said, 'An enemy has done this!'"* *"So, the slaves replied, 'Do you want us to go and gather it?'"* 29 *"But he said, 'No, since in gathering the darnel you may uproot the wheat along with it. 30 Let both grow together until the harvest. At harvest time I will tell the reapers: First collect the darnel and tie it in bundles to be burned; but then gather the wheat into my barn.'"*

The Parable of the Mustard Seed
Matthew 13:31-32

31 He gave them another parable: *"The kingdom of heaven is like a mustard seed that a man took and sowed in his field. 32 It is the smallest of all the seeds, but when it has grown it is the greatest garden plant and becomes a tree, so that the wild birds come and nest in its branches."*

The Parable of the Yeast
Matthew 13:33

33 He told them another parable: *"The kingdom of heaven is like yeast that a woman took and mixed with three measures of flour until all the dough had risen."*

The Purpose of Parables
Mathew 13:34-35

34 Jesus spoke all these things in parables to the crowds; he did not speak to them without a parable. 35 This fulfilled what was spoken by the prophet: "I will open my mouth in parables; I will announce what has been hidden from the foundation of the world."

The Parable of the Weeds Explained
-Galilee-
Matthew 13:36-43

36 Then he left the crowds and went into the house. And his disciples came to him saying, "Explain to us the parable of the darnel in the field." 37 He answered, *"The one who sowed the good seed is the Son of Man. 38 The field is the world and the good seed are the people of the kingdom. The poisonous weeds are the people of the evil one, 39 and the enemy who sows them is the devil. The harvest is the end of the age, and the reapers are angels. 40 As the poisonous weeds are collected and burned with fire, so it will be at the end of the age. 41 The Son of Man will send his angels, and they will gather from his kingdom everything that causes sin as well as all lawbreakers. 42 They will throw them into the fiery furnace, where there will be weeping and gnashing of teeth. 43 Then the righteous will shine like the sun in the kingdom of their Father. The one who has ears had better listen!"*

Jesus Teaches more Parables
-Galilee-
The Parable of the Hidden Treasure
Matthew 13:44

44 *"The kingdom of heaven is like a treasure, hidden in a field, that a person found and hid. Then because of joy he went and sold all that he had and bought that field."*

The Parable of Pearls
Matthew 13:45-46

45 *"Again, the kingdom of heaven is like a merchant searching for fine pearls. 46 When he found a pearl of great value, he went out and sold everything he had and bought it."*

The Parable of the Net
Matthew 13:47-52

47 *"Again, the kingdom of heaven is like a net that was cast into the sea that caught all kinds of fish. 48 When it was full, they pulled it ashore, sat down, and put the good fish into containers and threw the bad away. 49 It will be this way at the end of the age. Angels will come and separate the evil from the righteous 50 and throw them into the fiery furnace, where there will be weeping and gnashing of teeth.*

51 *"Have you understood all these things?"* They replied, "Yes." 52 Then he said to them, *"Therefore every expert in the law who has been trained for the kingdom of heaven is like the owner of a house who brings out of his treasure what is new and old."*

Many Similar Parables
Mark 4:33-34

33 So with many parables like these, he spoke the word to them, as they were able to hear. 34 He did not speak to them without a parable. But privately he explained everything to his own disciples.

Jesus Cams the Storm
-Sea of Galilee-
Matthew 13:53

53 Now when Jesus finished these parables, he moved on from there.

Mark 4:35-41

35 On that day, when evening came, Jesus said to his disciples, *"Let's go across to the other side of the lake."* 36 So after leaving the crowd, they took him along, just as he was, in the boat, and other boats were with him. 37 Now a great windstorm developed and the waves were breaking into the boat, so that the boat was nearly swamped. 38 But he was in the stern, sleeping on a cushion.

They woke him up and said to him, "Teacher, don't you care that we are about to die?" 39 So he got up and rebuked the wind, and said to the sea, *"Be quiet! Calm down!"* Then the wind stopped, and it was dead calm. 40 And he said to them, *"Why are you cowardly? Do you still not have faith?"* 41 They were overwhelmed by fear and said to one another, "Who then is this? Even the wind and sea obey him!"

The Two Demoniacs of Gadara
-South East Coast of the Sea of Galilee-
See Note: The Two Demoniacs
Matthew 8:28-29

28 When he came to the other side, to the region of the Gadarenes, two demon-possessed men coming from the tombs met him. They were extremely violent, so that no one was able to pass by that way. 29 They cried out, "Son of God, leave us alone! Have you come here to torment us before the time?"

Mark 5:3-20

3 He lived among the tombs, and no one could bind him anymore, not even with a chain. 4 For his hands and feet had often been bound with chains and shackles, but he had torn the chains apart and broken the shackles in pieces. No one was strong enough to subdue him. 5 Each night and every day among the tombs and in the mountains, he would cry out and cut himself with stones. 6 When he saw Jesus from a distance, he ran and bowed down before him. 7 Then he cried out with a loud voice, "Leave me alone, Jesus, Son of the Most High God! I implore you by God – do not torment me!" 8 (For Jesus had said to him, *"Come out of that man, you unclean spirit!"*) 9 Jesus asked him, *"What is your name?"* And he said, "My name is Legion, for we are many." 10 He begged Jesus repeatedly not to send them out of the region. 11 There on the hillside, a great herd of pigs was feeding. 12 And the demonic spirits begged him, "Send us into the pigs. Let us enter them." 13 Jesus gave them permission. So the unclean spirits came out and went into the pigs. Then the herd rushed down the steep slope into the lake, and about two thousand were drowned in the lake.

14 Now the herdsmen ran off and spread the news in the town and countryside, and the people went out to see what had happened. 15 They came to Jesus and saw the demon-possessed man sitting there, clothed and in his right mind – the one who had

the "Legion" – and they were afraid. 16 Those who had seen what had happened to the demon-possessed man reported it, and they also told about the pigs. 17 Then they began to beg Jesus to leave their region. 18 As he was getting into the boat the man who had been demon-possessed asked if he could go with him. 19 But Jesus did not permit him to do so. Instead, he said to him, *"Go to your home and to your people and tell them what the Lord has done for you, that he had mercy on you."* 20 So he went away and began to proclaim in the Decapolis what Jesus had done for him, and all were amazed.

Jesus Heals Jairus' Daughter and a Woman with an Issue of Blood
-Capernaum-
See Note: Jairus' Daughter
Luke 8:40-42

40 Now when Jesus returned, the crowd welcomed him, because they were all waiting for him. 41 Then a man named Jairus, who was a leader of the synagogue, came up. Falling at Jesus' feet, he pleaded with him to come to his house, 42 because he had an only daughter, about twelve years old, and she was dying. As Jesus was on his way, the crowds pressed around him.

Mark 5:25-43

25 Now a woman was there who had been suffering from a hemorrhage for twelve years. 26 She had endured a great deal under the care of many doctors and had spent all that she had. Yet instead of getting better, she grew worse. 27 When she heard about Jesus, she came up behind him in the crowd and touched his cloak, 28 for she kept saying, "If only I touch his clothes, I will be healed." 29 At once the bleeding stopped, and she felt in her body that she was healed of her disease. 30 Jesus knew at once that power had gone out from him. He turned around in the crowd and said, *"Who touched my clothes?"* 31 His disciples said to him, "You see the crowd pressing against you and you say, *'Who touched me?'"* 32 But he looked around to see who had done it. 33 Then the woman, with fear and trembling, knowing what had happened to her, came and fell down before him and told him the whole truth. 34 He said to her, *"Daughter, your faith has made you well. Go in peace, and be healed of your disease."*

35 While he was still speaking, people came from the synagogue leader's house saying, "Your daughter has died. Why trouble the

teacher any longer?" 36 But Jesus, paying no attention to what was said, told the synagogue leader, *"Do not be afraid; just believe."* 37 He did not let anyone follow him except Peter, James, and John, the brother of James. 38 They came to the house of the synagogue leader where he saw noisy confusion and people weeping and wailing loudly. 39 When he entered he said to them, *"Why are you distressed and weeping? The child is not dead but asleep!"* 40 And they began making fun of him. But he forced them all outside, and he took the child's father and mother and his own companions and went into the room where the child was. 41 Then, gently taking the child by the hand, he said to her, *"Talitha koum,"* which means, *"Little girl, I say to you, get up."* 42 The girl got up at once and began to walk around (she was twelve years old). They were completely astonished at this. 43 He strictly ordered that no one should know about this, and told them to give her something to eat.

Jesus Heals the Blind and Mute
-Probably Capernaum-
See Note: Blasphemy against the Holy Spirit
Matthew 9:27-34

27 As Jesus went on from there, two blind men began to follow him, shouting, "Have mercy on us, Son of David!" 28 When he went into the house, the blind men came to him. Jesus said to them, *"Do you believe that I am able to do this?"* They said to him, "Yes, Lord." 29 Then he touched their eyes saying, *"Let it be done for you according to your faith."* 30 And their eyes were opened. Then Jesus sternly warned them, *"See that no one knows about this!"* 31 But they went out and spread the news about him throughout that entire region.

32 As they were going away, a man who was demon-possessed and unable to speak was brought to him. 33 After the demon was cast out, the man who had been mute began to speak. The crowds were amazed and said, "Never has anything like this been seen in Israel!" 34 But the Pharisees said, "By the ruler of demons he casts out demons!"

A Prophet without Honor
-Nazareth-
See Note: Jesus' Brothers and Sisters
Mark 6:1-6

1 Now Jesus left that place and came to his hometown, and his disciples followed him. 2 When the Sabbath came, he began to teach in the synagogue. Many who heard him were astonished, saying, "Where did he get these ideas? And what is this wisdom that has been given to him? What are these miracles that are done through his hands? 3 Isn't this the carpenter, the son of Mary and brother of James, Joses, Judas, and Simon? And aren't his sisters here with us?" And so they took offense at him. 4 Then Jesus said to them, *"A prophet is not without honor except in his hometown, and among his relatives, and in his own house."* 5 He was not able to do a miracle there, except to lay his hands on a few sick people and heal them. 6 And he was amazed because of their unbelief. Then he went around among the villages and taught.

The Workers Are Few
-Galilee-
Matthew 9:35-38

35 Then Jesus went throughout all the towns and villages, teaching in their synagogues, preaching the good news of the kingdom, and healing every kind of disease and sickness. 36 When he saw the crowds, he had compassion on them because they were bewildered and helpless, like sheep without a shepherd. 37 Then he said to his disciples, *"The harvest is plentiful, but the workers are few. 38 Therefore ask the Lord of the harvest to send out workers into his harvest-ready fields."*

Jesus Sends Out the Twelve Apostles
-Galilee-
See Note: The Twelve Apostles
Matthew 10:1-33

1 Jesus called his twelve disciples and gave them authority over unclean spirits so they could cast them out and heal every kind of disease and sickness. 2 Now these are the names of the twelve apostles: first, Simon (called Peter), and Andrew his brother; James son of Zebedee and John his brother; 3 Philip and Bartholomew; Thomas and Matthew the tax collector; James the son of Alphaeus, and Thaddaeus; 4 Simon the Zealot and Judas Iscariot, who betrayed him.

5 Jesus sent out these twelve, instructing them as follows: *"Do not go on a road that leads to Gentile regions and do not enter any Samaritan town. 6 Go instead to the lost sheep of the house of*

Israel. *7 As you go, preach this message: 'The kingdom of heaven is near!' 8 Heal the sick, raise the dead, cleanse lepers, cast out demons. Freely you received, freely give. 9 Do not take gold, silver, or copper in your belts, 10 no bag for the journey, or an extra tunic, or sandals or staff, for the worker deserves his provisions."* 11 *"Whenever you enter a town or village, find out who is worthy there and stay with them until you leave. 12 As you enter the house, greet those within it. 13 And if the house is worthy, let your peace come on it, but if it is not worthy, let your peace return to you. 14 And if anyone will not welcome you or listen to your message, shake the dust off your feet as you leave that house or that town. 15 I tell you the truth; it will be more bearable for the region of Sodom and Gomorrah on the Day of Judgment than for that town!*

16 "I am sending you out like sheep surrounded by wolves, so be wise as serpents and innocent as doves." 17 "Beware of people, because they will hand you over to councils and flog you in their synagogues. 18 And you will be brought before governors and kings because of me, as a witness to them and to the Gentiles. 19 Whenever they hand you over for trial, do not worry about how to speak or what to say, for what you should say will be given to you at that time. 20 For it is not you speaking, but the Spirit of your Father speaking through you."

21 "Brother will hand over brother to death, and a father his child. Children will rise against parents and have them put to death. 22 And you will be hated by everyone because of my name. But the one who endures to the end will be saved! 23 Whenever they persecute you in one town, flee to another! I tell you the truth, you will not finish going through all the towns of Israel before the Son of Man comes."

24 "A disciple is not greater than his teacher, or a slave greater than his master. 25 It is enough for the disciple to become like his teacher, and the slave like his master. If they have called the head of the house 'Beelzebub,' how much worse will they call the members of his household?"

26 "Do not be afraid of them, for nothing is hidden that will not be revealed, and nothing is secret that will not be made known. 27 What I say to you in the dark, tell in the light, and what is whispered in your ear, proclaim from the housetops. 28 Do not be afraid of those who kill the body but cannot kill the soul. Instead, fear the one who is able to destroy both soul and body in hell. 29

Aren't two sparrows sold for a penny? Yet not one of them falls to the ground apart from your Father's will. 30 Even all the hairs on your head are numbered. 31 So do not be afraid; you are more valuable than many sparrows."

32 "Whoever, then, acknowledges me before people, I will acknowledge before my Father in heaven. 33 But whoever denies me before people, I will deny him also before my Father in heaven."

Luke 12:49-50

49 "I have come to bring fire on the earth – and how I wish it were already kindled! 50 I have a baptism to undergo, and how distressed I am until it is finished!"

Matthew 10:34-42

34 "Do not think that I have come to bring peace to the earth. I have not come to bring peace but a sword! 35 For I have come to set a man against his father, a daughter against her mother, and a daughter-in-law against her mother-in-law, 36 and a man's enemies will be the members of his household."

37 "Whoever loves father or mother more than me is not worthy of me, and whoever loves son or daughter more than me is not worthy of me. 38 And whoever does not take up his cross and follow me is not worthy of me. 39 Whoever finds his life will lose it, and whoever loses his life because of me will find it."

40 "Whoever receives you receives me, and whoever receives me receives the one who sent me. 41 Whoever receives a prophet in the name of a prophet will receive a prophet's reward. Whoever receives a righteous person in the name of a righteous person will receive a righteous person's reward. 42 And whoever gives only a cup of cold water to one of these little ones in the name of a disciple, I tell you the truth, he will never lose his reward."

Luke 12:10

10 "And everyone who speaks a word against the Son of Man will be forgiven, but the person who blasphemes against the Holy Spirit will not be forgiven."

Matthew 11:1

1. When Jesus had finished instructing his twelve disciples, he went on from there to teach and preach in their towns.

Mark 6:12-13

12 So they went out and preached that all should repent. 13 They cast out many demons and anointed many sick people with olive oil and healed them.

John the Baptist Beheaded
-Galilee-
Mark 6:14-29

14 Now King Herod heard this, for Jesus' name had become known. Some were saying, "John the baptizer has been raised from the dead, and because of this, miraculous powers are at work in him." 15 Others said, "He is Elijah." Others said, "He is a prophet, like one of the prophets from the past." 16 But when Herod heard this, he said, "John, whom I beheaded, has been raised!" 17 For Herod himself had sent men, arrested John, and bound him in prison on account of Herodias, his brother Philip's wife, because Herod had married her. 18 For John had repeatedly told Herod, "It is not lawful for you to have your brother's wife." 19 So Herodias nursed a grudge against him and wanted to kill him. But she could not 20 because Herod stood in awe of John and protected him, since he knew that John was a righteous and holy man. When Herod heard him, he was thoroughly baffled, and yet he liked to listen to John.

21 But a suitable day came, when Herod gave a banquet on his birthday for his court officials, military commanders, and leaders of Galilee. 22 When his daughter Herodias came in and danced, she pleased Herod and his dinner guests. The king said to the girl, "Ask me for whatever you want and I will give it to you." 23 He swore to her, "Whatever you ask I will give you, up to half my kingdom." 24 So she went out and said to her mother, "What should I ask for?" Her mother said, "The head of John the baptizer." 25 Immediately she hurried back to the king and made her request: "I want the head of John the Baptist on a platter immediately." 26 Although it grieved the king deeply, he did not want to reject her request because of his oath and his guests. 27 So the king sent an executioner at once to bring John's head, and he went and beheaded John in prison. 28 He brought his head on a platter and gave it to the girl, and the girl gave it to her mother. 29 When John's disciples heard this, they came and took his body and placed it in a tomb.

The Twelve Apostles Return
-Galilee-
Mark 6:30-31

30 Then the apostles gathered around Jesus and told him everything they had done and taught. 31 He said to them, *"Come with me privately to an isolated place and rest a while"* (for many were coming and going, and there was no time to eat).

Jesus Feeds the Five Thousand
-Bethsaida-
John 6:1-13

1 After this Jesus went away to the other side of the Sea of Galilee (also called the Sea of Tiberias). 2 A large crowd was following him because they were observing the miraculous signs he was performing on the sick. 3 So Jesus went on up the mountainside and sat down there with his disciples. 4 (Now the Jewish feast of the Passover was near.) 5 Then Jesus, when he looked up and saw that a large crowd was coming to him, said to Philip, *"Where can we buy bread so that these people may eat?"* 6 (Now Jesus said this to test him, for he knew what he was going to do.) 7 Philip replied, "Two hundred silver coins worth of bread would not be enough for them, for each one to get a little." 8 One of Jesus' disciples, Andrew, Simon Peter's brother, said to him, 9 "Here is a boy who has five barley loaves and two fish, but what good are these for so many people?"

10 Jesus said, *"Have the people sit down."* (Now there was a lot of grass in that place.) So the men sat down, about five thousand in number. 11 Then Jesus took the loaves, and when he had given thanks, he distributed the bread to those who were seated. He then did the same with the fish, as much as they wanted. 12 When they were all satisfied, Jesus said to his disciples, *"Gather up the broken pieces that are left over, so that nothing is wasted."* 13 So they gathered them up and filled twelve baskets with broken pieces from the five barley loaves left over by the people who had eaten.

Matthew 14:21

21 Not counting women and children, there were about five thousand men who ate.

Attempt to Make Jesus King
-Bethsaida-
John 6:14-15

14 Now when the people saw the miraculous sign that Jesus performed, they began to say to one another, "This is certainly the

Prophet who is to come into the world." 15 Then Jesus, because he knew they were going to come and seize him by force to make him king, withdrew again up the mountainside alone.

Jesus Walks on the Water
-Sea of Galilee-
John 6:16-17

16 Now when evening came, his disciples went down to the lake, 17 got into a boat, and started to cross the lake to Capernaum. (It had already become dark, and Jesus had not yet come to them.)

Matthew 14:24-31

24 Meanwhile the boat, already far from land, was taking a beating from the waves because the wind was against it. 25 As the night was ending, Jesus came to them walking on the sea. 26 When the disciples saw him walking on the water they were terrified and said, "It's a ghost!" and cried out with fear. 27 But immediately Jesus spoke to them: *"Have courage! It is I. Do not be afraid."* 28 Peter said to him, "Lord, if it is you, order me to come to you on the water." 29 So he said, *"Come."* Peter got out of the boat, walked on the water, and came toward Jesus. 30 But when he saw the strong wind he became afraid. And starting to sink, he cried out, "Lord, save me!" 31 Immediately Jesus reached out his hand and caught him, saying to him, *"You of little faith, why did you doubt?"*

Mark 6:51-52

51 Then he went up with them into the boat, and the wind ceased. They were completely astonished, 52 because they did not understand about the loaves, but their hearts were hardened.

Matthew 14:33

33 Then those who were in the boat worshiped him, saying, "Truly you are the Son of God."

Healings at Gennesaret
-Gennesaret-
Mark 6:53-56

53 After they had crossed over, they came to land at Gennesaret and anchored there. 54 As they got out of the boat, people immediately recognized Jesus. 55 They ran through that whole region and began to bring the sick on mats to wherever he was rumored to be. 56 And wherever he would go – into villages,

towns, or countryside – they would place the sick in the marketplaces, and would ask him if they could just touch the edge of his cloak, and all who touched it were healed.

Jesus the Bread of Life
-Capernaum-
John 6:22-59

22 The next day the crowd that remained on the other side of the lake realized that only one small boat had been there, and that Jesus had not boarded it with his disciples, but that his disciples had gone away alone. 23 Other boats from Tiberias came to shore near the place where they had eaten the bread after the Lord had given thanks. 24 So when the crowd realized that neither Jesus nor his disciples were there, they got into the boats and came to Capernaum looking for Jesus.

25 When they found him on the other side of the lake, they said to him, "Rabbi, when did you get here?" 26 Jesus replied, *"I tell you the solemn truth, you are looking for me not because you saw miraculous signs, but because you ate all the loaves of bread you wanted. 27 Do not work for the food that disappears, but for the food that remains to eternal life – the food which the Son of Man will give to you. For God the Father has put his seal of approval on him."*

28 So then they said to him, "What must we do to accomplish the deeds God requires?" 29 Jesus replied, *"This is the deed God requires – to believe in the one whom he sent."* 30 So they said to him, "Then what miraculous sign will you perform, so that we may see it and believe you? What will you do? 31 Our ancestors ate the manna in the wilderness, just as it is written, 'He gave them bread from heaven to eat.'"

32 Then Jesus told them, *"I tell you the solemn truth, it is not Moses who has given you the bread from heaven, but my Father is giving you the true bread from heaven. 33 For the bread of God is the one who comes down from heaven and gives life to the world."* 34 So they said to him, "Sir, give us this bread all the time!"

35 Jesus said to them, *"I am the bread of life. The one who comes to me will never go hungry, and the one who believes in me will never be thirsty. 36 But I told you that you have seen me and still do not believe. 37 Everyone whom the Father gives me will come to me, and the one who comes to me I will never send away. 38 For I have come down from heaven not to do my own will but*

the will of the one who sent me. *39 Now this is the will of the one who sent me – that I should not lose one person of every one he has given me, but raise them all up at the last day. 40 For this is the will of my Father – for everyone who looks on the Son and believes in him to have eternal life, and I will raise him up at the last day."*

41 Then the Jews who were hostile to Jesus began complaining about him because he said, *"I am the bread that came down from heaven,"* 42 and they said, "Isn't this Jesus the son of Joseph, whose father and mother we know? How can he now say, *'I have come down from heaven'?" 43 Jesus replied "Do not complain about me to one another. 44 No one can come to me unless the Father who sent me draws him, and I will raise him up at the last day. 45 It is written in the prophets, 'And they will all be taught by God.' Everyone who hears and learns from the Father comes to me. 46 (Not that anyone has seen the Father except the one who is from God – he has seen the Father.) 47 I tell you the solemn truth, the one who believes has eternal life. 48 I am the bread of life. 49 Your ancestors ate the manna in the wilderness, and they died. 50 This is the bread that has come down from heaven, so that a person may eat from it and not die. 51 I am the living bread that came down from heaven. If anyone eats from this bread he will live forever. The bread that I will give for the life of the world is my flesh."*

52 Then the Jews who were hostile to Jesus began to argue with one another, "How can this man give us his flesh to eat?" 53 Jesus said to them, *"I tell you the solemn truth, unless you eat the flesh of the Son of Man and drink his blood; you have no life in yourselves. 54 The one who eats my flesh and drinks my blood has eternal life, and I will raise him up on the last day. 55 For my flesh is true food, and my blood is true drink. 56 The one who eats my flesh and drinks my blood resides in me, and I in him. 57 Just as the living Father sent me, and I live because of the Father, so the one who consumes me will live because of me. 58 This is the bread that came down from heaven; it is not like the bread your ancestors ate, but then later died. The one who eats this bread will live forever."* 59 Jesus said these things while he was teaching in the synagogue in Capernaum.

Many Disciples Desert Jesus
-Capernaum-

60 Then many of his disciples, when they heard these things, said, "This is a difficult saying! Who can understand it?" 61 When Jesus was aware that his disciples were complaining about this, he said to them, *"Does this cause you to be offended? 62 Then what if you see the Son of Man ascending where he was before? 63 The Spirit is the one who gives life; human nature is of no help! The words that I have spoken to you are spirit and are life. 64 But there are some of you who do not believe."* (For Jesus had already known from the beginning who those were who did not believe, and who it was who would betray him.) 65 So Jesus added, *"Because of this I told you that no one can come to me unless the Father has allowed him to come."*

66 After this many of his disciples quit following him and did not accompany him any longer. 67 So Jesus said to the twelve, *"You don't want to go away too, do you?"* 68 Simon Peter answered him, "Lord, to whom would we go? You have the words of eternal life. 69 We have come to believe and to know that you are the Holy One of God!" 70 Jesus replied, *"Didn't I choose you, the twelve, and yet one of you is the devil?"* 71 (Now he said this about Judas son of Simon Iscariot, for Judas, one of the twelve, was going to betray him.)

John 7:1

1 After this Jesus traveled throughout Galilee. He stayed out of Judea because the Jewish leaders wanted to kill him.

Clean and Unclean
-Galilee, perhaps Capernaum-
Mark 7:1-5

1 Now the Pharisees and some of the experts in the law who came from Jerusalem gathered around him. 2 And they saw that some of Jesus' disciples ate their bread with unclean hands, that is, unwashed. 3 (For the Pharisees and all the Jews do not eat unless they perform a ritual washing, holding fast to the tradition of the elders. 4 And when they come from the marketplace, they do not eat unless they wash. They hold fast to many other traditions: the washing of cups, pots, kettles, and dining couches.) 5 The Pharisees and the experts in the law asked him, "Why do your disciples not live according to the tradition of the elders, but eat with unwashed hands?"

Matthew 15:3-18

3 He answered them, *"And why do you disobey the commandment of God because of your tradition? 4 For God said, 'Honor your father and mother' and 'whoever insults his father or mother must be put to death.' 5 But you say, 'If someone tells his father or mother, "Whatever help you would have received from me is given to God," 6 he does not need to honor his father.' You have nullified the word of God on account of your tradition. 7 Hypocrites! Isaiah prophesied correctly about you when he said, 8 'This people honor me with their lips, but their heart is far from me, 9 and they worship me in vain, teaching as doctrines the commandments of men.'"*

10 Then he called the crowd to him and said, *"Listen and understand. 11 What defiles a person is not what goes into the mouth; it is what comes out of the mouth that defiles a person."* 12 Then the disciples came to him and said, "Do you know that when the Pharisees heard this saying they were offended?" 13 And he replied, *"Every plant that my heavenly Father did not plant will be uprooted. 14 Leave them! They are blind guides. If someone who is blind leads another who is blind, both will fall into a pit."* 15 But Peter said to him, "Explain this parable to us." 16 Jesus said, *"Even after all this, are you still so foolish? 17 Don't you understand that whatever goes into the mouth enters the stomach and then passes out into the sewer? 18 But the things that come out of the mouth come from the heart, and these things defile a person."*

Mark 7:20-23

20 He said, *"What comes out of a person defiles him. 21 For from within, out of the human heart, come evil ideas, sexual immorality, theft, murder, 22 adultery, greed, evil, deceit, debauchery, envy, slander, pride, and folly. 23 All these evils come from within and defile a person."*

Matthew 15:20

20 *"These are the things that defile a person; it is not eating with unwashed hands that defile a person."*

Jesus Heals a Canaanite Women's Daughter
-Region of Tyre and Sidon-
Matthew 15:21-28

21 After going out from there, Jesus went to the region of Tyre and Sidon. 22 A Canaanite woman from that area came and cried out, "Have mercy on me, Lord, Son of David! My daughter is

horribly demon-possessed!" 23 But he did not answer her a word. Then his disciples came and begged him, "Send her away, because she keeps on crying out after us." 24 So he answered, *"I was sent only to the lost sheep of the house of Israel."* 25 But she came and bowed down before him and said, "Lord, help me!" 26 *"It is not right to take the children's bread and throw it to the dogs,"* he said. 27 "Yes, Lord," she replied, "but even the dogs eat the crumbs that fall from their masters' table." 28 Then Jesus answered her, *"Woman, your faith is great! Let what you want be done for you."* And her daughter was healed from that hour.

Mark 7:30

30 She went home and found the child lying on the bed, and the demon gone.

Healings in Decapolis
-In Decapolis near the Sea of Galilee-
Mark 7:31-37

31 Then Jesus went out again from the region of Tyre and came through Sidon to the Sea of Galilee in the region of the Decapolis. 32 They brought to him a deaf man who had difficulty speaking, and they asked him to place his hands on him. 33 After Jesus took him aside privately, away from the crowd, he put his fingers in the man's ears, and after spitting, he touched his tongue. 34 Then he looked up to heaven and said with a sigh, *"Ephphatha"* (that is, *"Be opened"*). 35 And immediately the man's ears were opened, his tongue loosened, and he spoke plainly. 36 Jesus ordered them not to tell anyone. But as much as he ordered them not to do this, they proclaimed it all the more. 37 People were completely astounded and said, "He has done everything well. He even makes the deaf hear and the mute speak."

Matthew 15:30-31

30 Then large crowds came to him bringing with them the lame, blind, crippled, mute, and many others. They laid them at his feet, and he healed them. 31 As a result, the crowd was amazed when they saw the mute speaking, the crippled healthy, the lame walking, and the blind seeing, and they praised the God of Israel.

Jesus Feeds the Four Thousand
-Decapolis-
Matthew 15-32-38

32 Then Jesus called the disciples and said, *"I have compassion on the crowd, because they have already been here with me three days and they have nothing to eat. I don't want to send them away hungry since they may faint on the way."* 33 The disciples said to him, "Where can we get enough bread in this desolate place to satisfy so great a crowd?" 34 Jesus said to them, *"How many loaves do you have?"* They replied, "Seven – and a few small fish." 35 After instructing the crowd to sit down on the ground, 36 he took the seven loaves and the fish, and after giving thanks, he broke them and began giving them to the disciples, who then gave them to the crowds. 37 They all ate and were satisfied, and they picked up the broken pieces left over, seven baskets full. 38 Not counting children and women, there were four thousand men who ate.

The Demand for a Sign
-Magadan-
Matthew 15:39-16:1-4

39 After sending away the crowd, he got into the boat and went to the region of Magadan.

16:1 Now when the Pharisees and Sadducees came to test Jesus, they asked him to show them a sign from heaven. 2 He said, *"When evening comes you say, 'It will be fair weather, because the sky is red,' 3 and in the morning, 'It will be stormy today, because the sky is red and darkening.' You know how to judge correctly the appearance of the sky, but you cannot evaluate the signs of the times. 4 A wicked and adulterous generation asks for a sign, but no sign will be given to it except the sign of Jonah."* Then he left them and went away.

The Yeast of the Pharisees and Sadducees
-Northeast Coast of the Sea of Galilee-
Mark 8:13-21

13 Then he left them, got back into the boat, and went to the other side.

14 Now they had forgotten to take bread, except for one loaf they had with them in the boat. 15 And Jesus ordered them, *"Watch out! Beware of the yeast of the Pharisees and the yeast of Herod!"* 16 So they began to discuss with one another about having no bread. 17 When he learned of this, Jesus said to them, *"Why are you arguing about having no bread? Do you still not*

see or understand? Have your hearts been hardened? 18 Though you have eyes, don't you see? And though you have ears, can't you hear? Don't you remember? 19 When I broke the five loaves for the five thousand, how many baskets full of pieces did you pick up?" They replied, "Twelve." *20 "When I broke the seven loaves for the four thousand, how many baskets full of pieces did you pick up?"* They replied, "Seven." 21 Then he said to them, *"Do you still not understand?"*

Matthew 16:12

12 Then they understood that he had not told them to be on guard against the yeast in bread, but against the teaching of the Pharisees and Sadducees.

The Healing of a Blind Man
-Bethsaida, Near Julias-
Mark 8:22-26

22 Then they came to Bethsaida. They brought a blind man to Jesus and asked him to touch him. 23 He took the blind man by the hand and brought him outside of the village. Then he spit on his eyes, placed his hands on his eyes and asked, *"Do you see anything?"* 24 Regaining his sight he said, "I see people, but they look like trees walking." 25 Then Jesus placed his hands on the man's eyes again. And he opened his eyes, his sight was restored, and he saw everything clearly. 26 Jesus sent him home, saying, *"Do not even go into the village."*

Peter's Confession of Christ
-District of Caesarea Philippi-
Matthew 16:13-20

13 When Jesus came to the area of Caesarea Philippi, he asked his disciples, *"Who do people say that the Son of Man is?"* 14 They answered, "Some say John the Baptist, others Elijah, and others Jeremiah or one of the prophets." 15 He said to them, *"But who do you say that I am?"* 16 Simon Peter answered, "You are the Christ, the Son of the living God." 17 And Jesus answered him, *"You are blessed, Simon son of Jonah, because flesh and blood did not reveal this to you, but my Father in heaven! 18 And I tell you that you are Peter, and on this rock, I will build my church, and the gates of Hades will not overpower it. 19 I will give you the keys of the kingdom of heaven. Whatever you bind on earth will have been bound in heaven, and whatever you release*

on earth will have been released in heaven." 20 Then he instructed his disciples not to tell anyone that he was the Christ.

Jesus Predicts His Death
-Near Caesarea Philippi-
Mark 8:31-9:1

31 Then Jesus began to teach them that the Son of Man must suffer many things and be rejected by the elders, chief priests, and experts in the law, and be killed, and after three days rise again. 32 He spoke openly about this. So Peter took him aside and began to rebuke him. 33 But after turning and looking at his disciples, he rebuked Peter and said, *"Get behind me, Satan. You are not setting your mind on God's interests, but on man's."*

34 Then Jesus called the crowd, along with his disciples, and said to them, *"If anyone wants to become my follower, he must deny himself, take up his cross, and follow me. 35 For whoever wants to save his life will lose it, but whoever loses his life because of me and because of the gospel will save it. 36 For what benefit is it for a person to gain the whole world, yet forfeit his life? 37 What can a person give in exchange for his life? 38 For if anyone is ashamed of me and my words in this adulterous and sinful generation, the Son of Man will also be ashamed of him when he comes in the glory of his Father with the holy angels."* 9:1 And he said to them, *"I tell you the truth, there are some standing here who will not experience death before they see the kingdom of God come with power."*

The Transfiguration of Jesus
-A high mountain, perhaps Mount Hermon-
Luke 9:28-33

28 Now about eight days after these sayings, Jesus took with him Peter, John, and James, and went up the mountain to pray. 29 As he was praying, the appearance of his face was transformed, and his clothes became very bright, a brilliant white. 30 Then two men, Moses and Elijah, began talking with him. 31 They appeared in glorious splendor and spoke about his departure that he was about to carry out at Jerusalem. 32 Now Peter and those with him were quite sleepy, but as they became fully awake, they saw his glory and the two men standing with him. 33 Then as the men were starting to leave, Peter said to Jesus, "Master, it is good for

us to be here. Let us make three shelters, one for you and one for Moses and one for Elijah" – not knowing what he was saying.

Matthew 17:5-8

5 While he was still speaking, a bright cloud enveloped them, and a voice from the cloud said, "This is my Son, whom I love; with him I am well pleased. Listen to him!" 6 When the disciples heard this, they fell facedown to the ground, terrified. 7 But Jesus came and touched them, *"Get up,"* he said. *"Don't be afraid."* 8 When they looked up, they saw no one except Jesus.

Mark 9:9-10

9 As they were coming down from the mountain, he gave them orders not to tell anyone what they had seen until after the Son of Man had risen from the dead. 10 They kept this statement to themselves, discussing what this rising from the dead meant.

Matthew 17:10-13

10 The disciples asked him, "Why then do the experts in the law say that Elijah must come first?" 11 He answered, *"Elijah does indeed come first and will restore all things. 12 And I tell you that Elijah has already come. Yet they did not recognize him, but did to him whatever they wanted. In the same way, the Son of Man will suffer at their hands."* 13 Then the disciples understood that he was speaking to them about John the Baptist.

The Healing of a Boy with an Evil Spirit
-Near the Mount of Transfiguration-
Mark 9:14-27

14 When they came to the disciples, they saw a large crowd around them and experts in the law arguing with them. 15 When the whole crowd saw him, they were amazed and ran at once and greeted him. 16 He asked them, *"What are you arguing about with them?"* 17 A member of the crowd said to him, "Teacher, I brought you my son, who is possessed by a spirit that makes him mute. 18 Whenever it seizes him, it throws him down, and he foams at the mouth, grinds his teeth, and becomes rigid. I asked your disciples to cast it out, but they were not able to do so." 19 He answered them, *"You unbelieving generation! How much longer must I be with you? How much longer must I endure you? Bring him to me."* 20 So they brought the boy to him. When the spirit saw him, it immediately threw the boy into a convulsion. He fell on the ground and rolled around, foaming at the mouth. 21 Jesus asked his father, *"How long has this been happening to*

him?" And he said, "From childhood. 22 It has often thrown him into fire or water to destroy him. But if you are able to do anything, have compassion on us and help us." 23 Then Jesus said to him, *"'If you are able?' All things are possible for the one who believes."* 24 Immediately the father of the boy cried out and said, "I believe; help my unbelief!"

25 Now when Jesus saw that a crowd was quickly gathering, he rebuked the unclean spirit, saying to it, *"Mute and deaf spirit, I command you, come out of him and never enter him again."* 26 It shrieked, threw him into terrible convulsions, and came out. The boy looked so much like a corpse that many said, "He is dead!" 27 But Jesus gently took his hand and raised him to his feet, and he stood up.

Matthew 17:19-20

19 Then the disciples came to Jesus privately and said, "Why couldn't we cast it out?" 20 He told them, *"It was because of your little faith. I tell you the truth, if you have faith the size of a mustard seed, you will say to this mountain, 'Move from here to there,' and it will move; nothing will be impossible for you."*

Again Jesus Teaches about His Death and Resurrection
-Itineration in Galilee-
Mark 9:30-32

30 They went out from there and passed through Galilee. But Jesus did not want anyone to know, 31 for he was teaching his disciples and telling them, *"The Son of Man will be betrayed into the hands of men. They will kill him, and after three days he will rise."* 32 But they did not understand this statement and were afraid to ask him.

The Temple Tax
-Capernaum-
Matthew 17:24-27

24 After they arrived in Capernaum, the collectors of the temple tax came to Peter and said, "Your teacher pays the double drachma tax, doesn't he?" 25 He said, "Yes." When Peter came into the house, Jesus spoke to him first, *"What do you think, Simon? From whom do earthly kings collect tolls or taxes – from their sons or from foreigners?"* 26 After he said, "From foreigners," Jesus said to him, *"Then the sons are free. 27 But so that we don't offend them, go to the lake and throw out a hook.*

Take the first fish that comes up, and when you open its mouth, you will find a four-drachma coin. Take that and give it to them for me and you."

The Greatest in the Kingdom of Heaven
-Capernaum-
Mark 9:33-36

33 Then they came to Capernaum. After Jesus was inside the house he asked them, *"What were you discussing on the way?"* 34 But they were silent, for on the way they had argued with one another about who was the greatest. 35 After he sat down, he called the twelve and said to them, *"If anyone wants to be first, he must be last of all and servant of all."* 36 He took a little child and had him stand among them. Taking him in his arms, he said to them,

Luke 9:48

48 *"Whoever welcomes this child in my name welcomes me, and whoever welcomes me welcomes the one who sent me, for the one who is least among you all is the one who is great."*

Whoever is Not against Us is for Us
-Capernaum-
Mark 9:38-41

38 John said to him, "Teacher, we saw someone casting out demons in your name, and we tried to stop him because he was not following us." 39 But Jesus said, *"Do not stop him, because no one who does a miracle in my name will be able soon afterward to say anything bad about me. 40 For whoever is not against us is for us. 41 For I tell you the truth, whoever gives you a cup of water because you bear Christ's name will never lose his reward."*

Causing to Sin
-Capernaum-
Mark 9:42

42 *"If anyone causes one of these little ones who believe in me to sin, it would be better for him to have a huge millstone tied around his neck and to be thrown into the sea."*

Matthew 18:7

7 *"Woe to the world because of stumbling blocks! It is necessary that stumbling blocks come, but woe to the person through whom they come."*

43 "If your hand causes you to sin, cut it off! It is better for you to enter into life crippled than to have two hands and go into hell, to the unquenchable fire. 45 If your foot causes you to sin, cut it off! It is better to enter life lame than to have two feet and be thrown into hell. 47 If your eye causes you to sin, tear it out! It is better to enter into the kingdom of God with one eye than to have two eyes and be thrown into hell, 48 where their worm never dies and the fire is never quenched. 49 Everyone will be salted with fire." 50 "Salt is good, but if it loses its saltiness, how can you make it salty again? Have salt in yourselves, and be at peace with each other."

The Parable of the Lost Sheep
-Capernaum-
See Note: Empty
Matthew 18:10-14

10 "See that you do not disdain one of these little ones. For I tell you that their angels in heaven always see the face of my Father in heaven." 11 [[EMPTY]] 12 "What do you think? If someone owns a hundred sheep and one of them goes astray, will he not leave the ninety-nine on the mountains and go look for the one that went astray? 13 And if he finds it, I tell you the truth, he will rejoice more over it than over the ninety-nine that did not go astray. 14 In the same way, your Father in heaven is not willing that one of these little ones be lost."

A Brother Who Sins Against You
-Capernaum-
Matthew 18:15-20

15 "If your brother sins, go and show him his fault when the two of you are alone. If he listens to you, you have regained your brother. 16 But if he does not listen, take one or two others with you, so that at the testimony of two or three witnesses every matter may be established. 17 If he refuses to listen to them, tell it to the church. If he refuses to listen to the church, treat him like a Gentile or a tax collector."

18 "I tell you the truth, whatever you bind on earth will have been bound in heaven, and whatever you release on earth will have been released in heaven." 19 "Again, I tell you the truth, if two of you on earth agree about whatever you ask, my Father in

Mark 9:43-50

43 "If your hand causes you to sin, cut it off! It is better for you to enter into life crippled than to have two hands and go into hell, to the unquenchable fire. 45 If your foot causes you to sin, cut it off! It is better to enter life lame than to have two feet and be thrown into hell. 47 If your eye causes you to sin, tear it out! It is better to enter into the kingdom of God with one eye than to have two eyes and be thrown into hell, 48 where their worm never dies and the fire is never quenched. 49 Everyone will be salted with fire." 50 "Salt is good, but if it loses its saltiness, how can you make it salty again? Have salt in yourselves, and be at peace with each other."

The Parable of the Lost Sheep
-Capernaum-
See Note: Empty
Matthew 18:10-14

10 "See that you do not disdain one of these little ones. For I tell you that their angels in heaven always see the face of my Father in heaven." 11 [[EMPTY]] 12 "What do you think? If someone owns a hundred sheep and one of them goes astray, will he not leave the ninety-nine on the mountains and go look for the one that went astray? 13 And if he finds it, I tell you the truth, he will rejoice more over it than over the ninety-nine that did not go astray. 14 In the same way, your Father in heaven is not willing that one of these little ones be lost."

A Brother Who Sins Against You
-Capernaum-
Matthew 18:15-20

15 "If your brother sins, go and show him his fault when the two of you are alone. If he listens to you, you have regained your brother. 16 But if he does not listen, take one or two others with you, so that at the testimony of two or three witnesses every matter may be established. 17 If he refuses to listen to them, tell it to the church. If he refuses to listen to the church, treat him like a Gentile or a tax collector."

18 "I tell you the truth, whatever you bind on earth will have been bound in heaven, and whatever you release on earth will have been released in heaven." 19 "Again, I tell you the truth, if two of you on earth agree about whatever you ask, my Father in

Take the first fish that comes up, and when you open its mouth, you will find a four-drachma coin. Take that and give it to them for me and you."

The Greatest in the Kingdom of Heaven
-Capernaum-
Mark 9:33-36

33 Then they came to Capernaum. After Jesus was inside the house he asked them, *"What were you discussing on the way?"* 34 But they were silent, for on the way they had argued with one another about who was the greatest. 35 After he sat down, he called the twelve and said to them, *"If anyone wants to be first, he must be last of all and servant of all."* 36 He took a little child and had him stand among them. Taking him in his arms, he said to them,

Luke 9:48

48 *"Whoever welcomes this child in my name welcomes me, and whoever welcomes me welcomes the one who sent me, for the one who is least among you all is the one who is great."*

Whoever is Not against Us is for Us
-Capernaum-
Mark 9:38-41

38 John said to him, "Teacher, we saw someone casting out demons in your name, and we tried to stop him because he was not following us." 39 But Jesus said, *"Do not stop him, because no one who does a miracle in my name will be able soon afterward to say anything bad about me. 40 For whoever is not against us is for us. 41 For I tell you the truth, whoever gives you a cup of water because you bear Christ's name will never lose his reward."*

Causing to Sin
-Capernaum-
Mark 9:42

42 *"If anyone causes one of these little ones who believe in me to sin, it would be better for him to have a huge millstone tied around his neck and to be thrown into the sea."*

Matthew 18:7

7 *"Woe to the world because of stumbling blocks! It is necessary that stumbling blocks come, but woe to the person through whom they come."*

heaven will do it for you. 20 For where two or three are assembled in my name, I am there among them."

The Parable of the Unmerciful Servant
-Capernaum-
Matthew 18:21-35

21 Then Peter came to him and said, "Lord, how many times must I forgive my brother who sins against me? As many as seven times?" 22 Jesus said to him, *"Not seven times, I tell you, but seventy-seven times!"*

23 *"For this reason, the kingdom of heaven is like a king who wanted to settle accounts with his slaves. 24 As he began settling his accounts, a man who owed ten thousand talents was brought to him. 25 Because he was not able to repay it, the lord ordered him to be sold, along with his wife, children, and whatever he possessed, and repayment to be made." 26 "Then the slave threw himself to the ground before him, saying, 'Be patient with me, and I will repay you everything.' 27 The lord had compassion on that slave and released him, and forgave him the debt." 28 "After he went out, that same slave found one of his fellow slaves who owed him one hundred silver coins. So, he grabbed him by the throat and started to choke him, saying, 'Pay back what you owe me!'" 29 "Then his fellow slave threw himself down and begged him, 'Be patient with me, and I will repay you.'" 30 "But he refused. Instead, he went out and threw him in prison until he repaid the debt. 31 When his fellow slaves saw what had happened, they were very upset and went and told their lord everything that had taken place." 32 "Then his lord called the first slave and said to him, 'Evil slave! I forgave you all that debt because you begged me! 33 Should you not have shown mercy to your fellow slave, just as I showed it to you?' 34 And in anger his lord turned him over to the prison guards to torture him until he repaid all he owed." 35 "So also my heavenly Father will do to you, if each of you does not forgive your brother from your heart."*

Ridicule by Jesus' Half-Brothers
-Galilee-
See Note: Jesus' Brothers and Sisters
John 7:2-10

2 Now the Jewish feast of Tabernacles was near. 3 So Jesus' brothers advised him, "Leave here and go to Judea so your

disciples may see your miracles that you are performing. 4 For no one who seeks to make a reputation for himself does anything in secret. If you are doing these things, show yourself to the world." 5 (For not even his own brothers believed in him.)

6 So Jesus replied, *"My time has not yet arrived, but you are ready at any opportunity! 7 The world cannot hate you, but it hates me, because I am testifying about it that its deeds are evil. 8 You go up to the feast yourselves. I am not going up to this feast because my time has not yet fully arrived."* 9 When he had said this, he remained in Galilee.

10 But when his brothers had gone up to the feast, then Jesus himself also went up, not openly but in secret.

Journey through Samaria
-Start of Journey to Jerusalem-
Luke 9:51-56

51 Now when the days drew near for him to be taken up, Jesus set out resolutely to go to Jerusalem. 52 He sent messengers on ahead of him. As they went along, they entered a Samaritan village to make things ready in advance for him, 53 but the villagers refused to welcome him, because he was determined to go to Jerusalem. 54 Now when his disciples James and John saw this, they said, "Lord, do you want us to call fire to come down from heaven and consume them?" 55 But Jesus turned and rebuked them, 56 and they went on to another village.

The Cost of Following Jesus
-On the Road-
Luke 9:57-62

57 As they were walking along the road, someone said to him, "I will follow you wherever you go." 58 Jesus said to him, *"Foxes have dens and the birds in the sky have nests, but the Son of Man has no place to lay his head."* 59 Jesus said to another, *"Follow me."* But he replied, "Lord, first let me go and bury my father." 60 But Jesus said to him, *"Let the dead bury their own dead, but as for you, go and proclaim the kingdom of God."* 61 Yet another said, "I will follow you, Lord, but first let me say goodbye to my family." 62 Jesus said to him, *"No one who puts his hand to the plow and looks back is fit for the kingdom of God."*

Jesus Teaches at the Feast

11 So the Jewish leaders were looking for him at the feast, asking, "Where is he?" 12 There was a lot of grumbling about him among the crowds. Some were saying, "He is a good man," But others, "He deceives the common people." 13 However, no one spoke openly about him for fear of the Jewish leaders.

14 When the feast was half over, Jesus went up to the temple courts and began to teach. 15 Then the Jewish leaders were astonished and said, "How does this man know so much when he has never had formal instruction?" 16 So Jesus replied, *"My teaching is not from me, but from the one who sent me. 17 If anyone wants to do God's will, he will know about my teaching, whether it is from God or whether I speak from my own authority. 18 The person who speaks on his own authority desires to receive honor for himself; the one who desires the honor of the one who sent him is a man of integrity, and there is no unrighteousness in him. 19 Hasn't Moses given you the law? Yet not one of you keeps the law! Why do you want to kill me?"*

20 The crowd answered, "You're possessed by a demon! Who is trying to kill you?" 21 Jesus replied, *"I performed one miracle and you are all amazed. 22 However, because Moses gave you the practice of circumcision (not that it came from Moses, but from the forefathers), you circumcise a male child on the Sabbath. 23 But if a male child is circumcised on the Sabbath so that the Law of Moses is not broken, why are you angry with me because I made a man completely well on the Sabbath? 24 Do not judge according to external appearance, but judge with proper judgment."*

25 Then some of the residents of Jerusalem began to say, "Isn't this the man they are trying to kill? 26 Yet here he is, speaking publicly, and they are saying nothing to him. Do the ruling authorities really know that this man is the Christ? 27 But we know where this man comes from. Whenever the Christ comes, no one will know where he comes from."

28 Then Jesus, while teaching in the temple courts, cried out, *"You both know me and know where I come from! And I have not come on my own initiative, but the one who sent me is true. You do not know him, 29 but I know him, because I have come from him and he sent me."*

30 So then they tried to seize Jesus, but no one laid a hand on him, because his time had not yet come. 31 Yet many of the crowd believed in him and said, "Whenever the Christ comes, he won't perform more miraculous signs than this man did, will he?"

Frustrated Attempt to Arrest Jesus
-Jerusalem-
John 7:32-52

32 The Pharisees heard the crowd murmuring these things about Jesus, so the chief priests and the Pharisees sent officers to arrest him. 33 Then Jesus said, *"I will be with you for only a little while longer, and then I am going to the one who sent me. 34 You will look for me but will not find me, and where I am you cannot come."*

35 Then the Jewish leaders said to one another, "Where is he going to go that we cannot find him? He is not going to go to the Jewish people dispersed among the Greeks and teach the Greeks, is he? 36 What did he mean by saying, *'You will look for me but will not find me, and where I am you cannot come'?"*

37 On the last day of the feast, the greatest day, Jesus stood up and shouted out, *"If anyone is thirsty, let him come to me, and 38 let the one who believes in me drink. Just as the scripture says, 'from within him will flow rivers of living water.'"* 39 (Now he said this about the Spirit, whom those who believed in him were going to receive, for the Spirit had not yet been given, because Jesus was not yet glorified.)

40 When they heard these words, some of the crowd began to say, "This really is the Prophet!" 41 Others said, "This is the Christ!" But still others said, "No, for the Christ doesn't come from Galilee, does he? 42 Don't the scriptures say that the Christ is a descendant of David and comes from Bethlehem, the village where David lived?" 43 So there was a division in the crowd because of Jesus. 44 Some of them were wanting to seize him, but no one laid a hand on him.

45 Then the officers returned to the chief priests and Pharisees, who said to them, "Why didn't you bring him back with you?" 46 The officers replied, "No one ever spoke like this man!" 47 Then the Pharisees answered, "You haven't been deceived too, have you? 48 None of the members of the ruling council or the Pharisees have believed in him, have they? 49 But this rabble who do not know the law are accursed!"

50 Nicodemus, who had gone to Jesus before and who was one of the rulers, said, 51 "Our law doesn't condemn a man unless it first hears from him and learns what he is doing, does it?" 52 They replied, "You aren't from Galilee too, are you? Investigate carefully and you will see that no prophet comes from Galilee!"

Jesus Forgiveness of an Adulteress
-Jerusalem, in the Temple-
John 7:53-8:1-11

53 And each one departed to his own house. 1 But Jesus went to the Mount of Olives. 2 Early in the morning he came to the temple courts again. All the people came to him, and he sat down and began to teach them. 3 The experts in the law and the Pharisees brought a woman who had been caught committing adultery. They made her stand in front of them 4 and said to Jesus, "Teacher, this woman was caught in the very act of adultery. 5 In the law Moses commanded us to stone to death such women. What then do you say?" 6 (Now they were asking this in an attempt to trap him, so that they could bring charges against him.) Jesus bent down and wrote on the ground with his finger. 7 When they persisted in asking him, he stood up straight and replied, *"Whoever among you is guiltless may be the first to throw a stone at her."* 8 Then he bent over again and wrote on the ground.

9 Now when they heard this, they began to drift away one at a time, starting with the older ones, until Jesus was left alone with the woman standing before him. 10 Jesus stood up straight and said to her, *"Woman, where are they? Did no one condemn you?"* 11 She replied, "No one, Lord." And Jesus said, *"I do not condemn you either. Go, and from now on do not sin anymore."*

The Validity of Jesus' Testimony
-Jerusalem in the Temple-
John 8:12-20

12 Then Jesus spoke out again, *"I am the light of the world! The one who follows me will never walk in darkness, but will have the light of life."* 13 So the Pharisees objected, "You testify about yourself; your testimony is not true!" 14 Jesus answered, *"Even if I testify about myself, my testimony is true, because I know where I came from and where I am going. But you people do not know where I came from or where I am going. 15 You people judge by outward appearances; I do not judge anyone. 16 But if I judge, my*

evaluation is accurate, because I am not alone when I judge, but I and the Father who sent me do so together. 17 It is written in your law that the testimony of two men is true. 18 I testify about myself and the Father who sent me testifies about me."

19 Then they began asking him, "Who is your father?" Jesus answered, *"You do not know either me or my Father. If you knew me you would know my Father too."* 20 (Jesus spoke these words near the offering box while he was teaching in the temple courts. No one seized him because his time had not yet come.)

Invitation to Believe in Jesus
-Jerusalem, in the Temple-
John 8:21-30

21 Then Jesus said to them again, *"I am going away, and you will look for me but will die in your sin. Where I am going you cannot come."* 22 So the Jewish leaders began to say, "Perhaps he is going to kill himself, because he says, *'Where I am going you cannot come.'"* 23 Jesus replied, *"You people are from below; I am from above. You people are from this world; I am not from this world. 24 Thus I told you that you will die in your sins. For unless you believe that I am he, you will die in your sins."*

25 So they said to him, "Who are you?" Jesus replied, *"What I have told you from the beginning. 26 I have many things to say and to judge about you, but the Father who sent me is truthful, and the things I have heard from him I speak to the world."* 27 (They did not understand that he was telling them about his Father.)

28 Then Jesus said, *"When you lift up the Son of Man, then you will know that I am he, and I do nothing on my own initiative, but I speak just what the Father taught me. 29 And the one who sent me is with me. He has not left me alone, because I always do those things that please him."* 30 While he was saying these things, many people believed in him.

The Children of Abraham
-Jerusalem, in the Temple-
John 8:31-41

31 Then Jesus said to those Judeans who had believed him, *"If you continue to follow my teaching, you are really my disciples 32 and you will know the truth, and the truth will set you free."* 33 "We are descendants of Abraham," they replied, "and have never been anyone's slaves! How can you say, 'You will become free'?"

34 Jesus answered them, *"I tell you the solemn truth, everyone who practices sin is a slave of sin. 35 The slave does not remain in the family forever, but the son remains forever. 36 So if the son sets you free, you will be really free. 37 I know that you are Abraham's descendants. But you want to kill me, because my teaching makes no progress among you. 38 I am telling you the things I have seen while with the Father; as for you, practice the things you have heard from the Father!"*

39 They answered him, "Abraham is our father!" Jesus replied, *"If you are Abraham's children, you would be doing the deeds of Abraham. 40 But now you are trying to kill me, a man who has told you the truth I heard from God. Abraham did not do this! 41 You people are doing the deeds of your father."*

Then they said to Jesus, "We were not born as a result of immorality! We have only one Father, God himself."

The Children of the Devil
-Jerusalem, in the Temple-
John 8:42-47

42 Jesus replied, *"If God were your Father, you would love me, for I have come from God and am now here. I have not come on my own initiative, but he sent me. 43 Why don't you understand what I am saying? It is because you cannot accept my teaching. 44 You people are from your father the devil, and you want to do what your father desires. He was a murderer from the beginning, and does not uphold the truth, because there is no truth in him. Whenever he lies, he speaks according to his own nature, because he is a liar and the father of lies. 45 But because I am telling you the truth, you do not believe me. 46 Who among you can prove me guilty of any sin? If I am telling you the truth, why don't you believe me? 47 The one who belongs to God listens and responds to God's words. You don't listen and respond, because you don't belong to God."*

The Claims of Jesus about Himself
-Jerusalem, in the Temple-
John 8:48-59

48 The Judeans replied, "Aren't we correct in saying that you are a Samaritan and are possessed by a demon?" 49 Jesus answered, *"I am not possessed by a demon, but I honor my Father – and yet you dishonor me. 50 I am not trying to get praise for*

myself. There is one who demands it, and he also judges. 51 I tell you the solemn truth, if anyone obeys my teaching, he will never see death."

52 Then the Judeans responded; "Now we know you're possessed by a demon! Both Abraham and the prophets died, and yet you say, 'If anyone obeys my teaching, he will never experience death.' 53 You aren't greater than our father Abraham who died, are you? And the prophets died too! Who do you claim to be?" 54 Jesus replied, *"If I glorify myself, my glory is worthless. The one who glorifies me is my Father, about whom you people say, 'He is our God.' 55 Yet you do not know him, but I know him. If I were to say that I do not know him, I would be a liar like you. But I do know him, and I obey his teaching. 56 Your father Abraham was overjoyed to see my day, and he saw it and was glad."*

57 Then the Judeans replied, "You are not yet fifty years old! Have you seen Abraham?" 58 Jesus said to them, *"I tell you the solemn truth, before Abraham came into existence, I am!"* 59 Then they picked up stones to throw at him, but Jesus was hidden from them and went out from the temple area.

Jesus Sends Out the Seventy-Two
-Probably in Judea-
Luke 10:1-16

1 After this the Lord appointed seventy-two others and sent them on ahead of him two by two into every town and place where he himself was about to go. 2 He said to them, *"The harvest is plentiful, but the workers are few. Therefore, ask the Lord of the harvest to send out workers into his harvest. 3 Go! I am sending you out like lambs surrounded by wolves. 4 Do not carry a money bag, a traveler's bag, or sandals, and greet no one on the road." 5 "Whenever you enter a house, first say, 'May peace be on this house!' 6 And if a peace-loving person is there, your peace will remain on him, but if not, it will return to you. 7 Stay in that same house, eating and drinking what they give you, for the worker deserves his pay. Do not move around from house to house. 8 Whenever you enter a town and the people welcome you, eat what is set before you. 9 Heal the sick in that town and say to them, 'The kingdom of God has come upon you!' 10 But whenever you enter a town and the people do not welcome you, go into its streets and say, 11 'Even the dust of your town that clings to our feet we*

wipe off against you. Nevertheless, know this: The kingdom of God has come.' 12 I tell you, it will be more bearable on that day for Sodom than for that town!"

13 "Woe to you, Chorazin! Woe to you, Bethsaida! For if the miracles done in you had been done in Tyre and Sidon, they would have repented long ago, sitting in sackcloth and ashes. 14 But it will be more bearable for Tyre and Sidon in the judgment than for you! 15 And you, Capernaum, will you be exalted to heaven? No, you will be thrown down to Hades!"

16 "The one who listens to you listens to me, and the one who rejects you rejects me, and the one who rejects me rejects the one who sent me."

Return of the Seventy-Two
-Probably in Judea-
Luke 10:17-24

17 Then the seventy-two returned with joy, saying, "Lord, even the demons submit to us in your name!" 18 So he said to them, *"I saw Satan fall like lightning from heaven. 19 Look, I have given you authority to tread on snakes and scorpions and on the full force of the enemy, and nothing will hurt you. 20 Nevertheless, do not rejoice that the spirits submit to you, but rejoice that your names stand written in heaven."*

21 On that same occasion Jesus rejoiced in the Holy Spirit and said, *"I praise you, Father, Lord of heaven and earth, because you have hidden these things from the wise and intelligent, and revealed them to little children. Yes, Father, for this was your gracious will." 22 "All things have been given to me by my Father. No one knows who the Son is except the Father, or who the Father is except the Son and anyone to whom the Son decides to reveal him."*

23 Then Jesus turned to his disciples and said privately, *"Blessed are the eyes that see what you see! 24 For I tell you that many prophets and kings longed to see what you see but did not see it, and to hear what you hear but did not hear it."*

The Parable of the Good Samaritan
-Probably in Judea-
Luke 10:25-37

25 Now an expert in religious law stood up to test Jesus, saying, "Teacher, what must I do to inherit eternal life?" 26 He said to

him, *"What is written in the law? How do you understand it?"* 27 The expert answered, "Love the Lord your God with all your heart, with all your soul, with all your strength, and with all your mind, and love your neighbor as yourself." 28 Jesus said to him, *"You have answered correctly; do this, and you will live."*

29 But the expert, wanting to justify himself, said to Jesus, "And who is my neighbor?" 30 Jesus replied, *"A man was going down from Jerusalem to Jericho, and fell into the hands of robbers, who stripped him, beat him up, and went off, leaving him half dead. 31 Now by chance a priest was going down that road, but when he saw the injured man he passed by on the other side. 32 So too a Levite, when he came up to the place and saw him, passed by on the other side. 33 But a Samaritan who was traveling came to where the injured man was, and when he saw him, he felt compassion for him. 34 He went up to him and bandaged his wounds, pouring olive oil and wine on them. Then he put him on his own animal, brought him to an inn, and took care of him. 35 The next day he took out two silver coins and gave them to the innkeeper, saying, 'Take care of him, and whatever else you spend, I will repay you when I come back this way.'" 36 "Which of these three do you think became a neighbor to the man who fell into the hands of the robbers?"* 37 The expert in religious law said, "The one who showed mercy to him." So, Jesus said to him, *"Go and do the same."*

Jesus' Visit with Mary and Martha
-Bethany near Jerusalem-
Luke 10:38-42

38 Now as they went on their way, Jesus entered a certain village where a woman named Martha welcomed him as a guest. 39 She had a sister named Mary, who sat at the Lord's feet and listened to what he said. 40 But Martha was distracted with all the preparations she had to make, so she came up to him and said, "Lord, don't you care that my sister has left me to do all the work alone? Tell her to help me." 41 But the Lord answered her, *"Martha, Martha, you are worried and troubled about many things, 42 but one thing is needed. Mary has chosen the best part; it will not be taken away from her."*

Jesus' Teaching on Prayer
-Near Jerusalem-

1 Now Jesus was praying in a certain place. When he stopped, one of his disciples said to him, "Lord, teach us to pray, just as John taught his disciples." 2 So he said to them, *"When you pray, say: Father, may your name be honored; may your kingdom come. 3 Give us each day our daily bread, 4 and forgive us our sins, for we also forgive everyone who sins against us. And do not lead us into temptation."*

5 Then he said to them, *"Suppose one of you has a friend, and you go to him at midnight and say to him, 'Friend, lend me three loaves of bread, 6 because a friend of mine has stopped here while on a journey, and I have nothing to set before him.'"* 7 *"Then he will reply from inside, 'Do not bother me. The door is already shut, and my children and I are in bed. I cannot get up and give you anything.' 8 I tell you, even though the man inside will not get up and give him anything because he is his friend, yet because of the first man's sheer persistence he will get up and give him whatever he needs."*

9 *"So I tell you: Ask, and it will be given to you; seek, and you will find; knock, and the door will be opened for you. 10 For everyone who asks receives, and the one who seeks finds, and to the one who knocks, the door will be opened."* 11 *"What father among you, if your son asks for a fish, will give him a snake instead of a fish? 12 Or if he asks for an egg, will give him a scorpion? 13 If you then, although you are evil, know how to give good gifts to your children, how much more will the heavenly Father give the Holy Spirit to those who ask him!"*

The Parable of the Rich Fool
-Probably in Judea-
Luke 12:13-21

13 Then someone from the crowd said to him, "Teacher, tell my brother to divide the inheritance with me." 14 But Jesus said to him, *"Man, who made me a judge or arbitrator between you two?"* 15 Then he said to them, *"Watch out and guard yourself from all types of greed, because one's life does not consist in the abundance of his possessions."* 16 He then told them a parable: *"The land of a certain rich man produced an abundant crop, 17 so he thought to himself, 'What should I do, for I have nowhere to store my crops?'"* 18 *"Then he said, 'I will do this: I will tear down my barns and build bigger ones, and there I will store all my*

grain and my goods. 19 And I will say to myself, "You have plenty of goods stored up for many years; relax, eat, drink, celebrate!"' 20 "But God said to him, 'You fool! This very night your life will be demanded back from you, but who will get what you have prepared for yourself?' 21 So it is with the one who stores up riches for himself, but is not rich toward God."

Watchfulness
-Probably in Judea-
Luke 12:35-48

35 "Get dressed for service and keep your lamps burning; 36 be like people waiting for their master to come back from the wedding celebration, so that when he comes and knocks they can immediately open the door for him. 37 Blessed are those slaves whom their master finds alert when he returns! I tell you the truth, he will dress himself to serve, have them take their place at the table, and will come and wait on them! 38 Even if he comes in the second or third watch of the night and finds them alert, blessed are those slaves! 39 But understand this: If the owner of the house had known at what hour the thief was coming, he would not have let his house be broken into. 40 You also must be ready, because the Son of Man will come at an hour when you do not expect him."

41 Then Peter said, "Lord, are you telling this parable for us or for everyone?" 42 The Lord replied, *"Who then is the faithful and wise manager, whom the master puts in charge of his household servants, to give them their allowance of food at the proper time? 43 Blessed is that slave whom his master finds at work when he returns. 44 I tell you the truth; the master will put him in charge of all his possessions. 45 But if that slave should say to himself, 'My master is delayed in returning,' and he begins to beat the other slaves, both men and women, and to eat, drink, and get drunk, 46 then the master of that slave will come on a day when he does not expect him and at an hour he does not foresee, and will cut him in two, and assign him a place with the unfaithful." 47 "That servant who knew his master's will but did not get ready or do what his master asked will receive a severe beating. 48 But the one who did not know his master's will and did things worthy of punishment will receive a light beating. From everyone who has been given much, much will be required, and from the one who has been entrusted with much, even more will be asked."*

Interpreting the Times
-Probably in Judea-
Luke 12:54-59

54 Jesus also said to the crowds, *"When you see a cloud rising in the west, you say at once, 'A rainstorm is coming,' and it does. 55 And when you see the south wind blowing, you say, 'There will be scorching heat,' and there is. 56 You hypocrites! You know how to interpret the appearance of the earth and the sky, but how can you not know how to interpret the present time?"*

57 *"And why don't you judge for yourselves what is right? 58 As you are going with your accuser before the magistrate, make an effort to settle with him on the way, so that he will not drag you before the judge, and the judge hand you over to the officer, and the officer throw you into prison. 59 I tell you, you will never get out of there until you have paid the very last cent!"*

Repent or Perish
-Probably in Judea-
Luke 13:1-9

1 Now there were some present on that occasion who told him about the Galileans whose blood Pilate had mixed with their sacrifices. 2 He answered them, *"Do you think these Galileans were worse sinners than all the other Galileans, because they suffered these things? 3 No, I tell you! But unless you repent, you will all perish as well! 4 Or those eighteen who were killed when the tower in Siloam fell on them, do you think they were worse offenders than all the others who live in Jerusalem? 5 No, I tell you! But unless you repent you will all perish as well!"*

6 Then Jesus told this parable: *"A man had a fig tree planted in his vineyard, and he came looking for fruit on it and found none. 7 So he said to the worker who tended the vineyard, 'For three years now, I have come looking for fruit on this fig tree, and each time I inspect it I find none. Cut it down! Why should it continue to deplete the soil?'" 8 "But the worker answered him, 'Sir, leave it alone this year too, until I dig around it and put fertilizer on it. 9 Then if it bears fruit next year, very well, but if not, you can cut it down.'"*

A Crippled Woman Healed on the Sabbath
-Probably in Judea-
Luke 13:10-17

10 Now he was teaching in one of the synagogues on the Sabbath, 11 and a woman was there who had been disabled by a spirit for eighteen years. She was bent over and could not straighten herself up completely. 12 When Jesus saw her, he called her to him and said, *"Woman, you are freed from your infirmity."* 13 Then he placed his hands on her, and immediately she straightened up and praised God. 14 But the president of the synagogue, indignant because Jesus had healed on the Sabbath, said to the crowd, "There are six days on which work should be done! So, come and be healed on those days, and not on the Sabbath day." 15 Then the Lord answered him, *"You hypocrites! Does not each of you on the Sabbath untie his ox or his donkey from its stall, and lead it to water? 16 Then shouldn't this woman, a daughter of Abraham whom Satan bound for eighteen long years, be released from this imprisonment on the Sabbath day?"* 17 When he said this all his adversaries were humiliated, but the entire crowd was rejoicing at all the wonderful things he was doing.

Jesus Heals a Man Born Blind
-Jerusalem-
John 9:1-12

1 Now as Jesus was passing by, he saw a man who had been blind from birth. 2 His disciples asked him, "Rabbi, who committed the sin that caused him to be born blind, this man or his parents?" 3 Jesus answered, *"Neither this man nor his parents sinned, but he was born blind so that the acts of God may be revealed through what happens to him. 4 We must perform the deeds of the one who sent me as long as it is daytime. Night is coming when no one can work. 5 As long as I am in the world, I am the light of the world."* 6 Having said this, he spat on the ground and made some mud with the saliva. He smeared the mud on the blind man's eyes 7 and said to him, *"Go wash in the pool of Siloam"* (which is translated "sent"). So the blind man went away and washed, and came back seeing.

8 Then the neighbors and the people who had seen him previously as a beggar began saying, "Is this not the man who used to sit and beg?" 9 Some people said, "This is the man!" while others said, "No, but he looks like him." The man himself kept insisting, "I am the one!" 10 So they asked him, "How then were

you made to see?" 11 He replied, "The man called Jesus made mud, smeared it on my eyes and told me, 'Go to Siloam and wash.' So I went and washed, and was able to see." 12 They said to him, "Where is that man?" He replied, "I don't know."

The Pharisees Investigate the Healing
-Jerusalem-
John 9:13-34

13 They brought the man who used to be blind to the Pharisees. 14 (Now the day on which Jesus made the mud and caused him to see was a Sabbath.) 15 So the Pharisees asked him again how he had gained his sight. He replied, "He put mud on my eyes and I washed, and now I am able to see."

16 Then some of the Pharisees began to say, "This man is not from God, because he does not observe the Sabbath." But others said, "How can a man who is a sinner perform such miraculous signs?" Thus there was a division among them. 17 So again they asked the man who used to be blind, "What do you say about him, since he caused you to see?" "He is a prophet," the man replied.

18 Now the Jewish religious leaders refused to believe that he had really been blind and had gained his sight until at last they summoned the parents of the man who had become able to see. 19 They asked the parents, "Is this your son, whom you say was born blind? Then how does he now see?" 20 So his parents replied, "We know that this is our son and that he was born blind. 21 But we do not know how he is now able to see, nor do we know who caused him to see. Ask him, he is a mature adult. He will speak for himself." 22 (His parents said these things because they were afraid of the Jewish religious leaders. For the Jewish leaders had already agreed that anyone who confessed Jesus to be the Christ would be put out of the synagogue. 23 For this reason his parents said, "He is a mature adult, ask him.")

24 Then they summoned the man who used to be blind a second time and said to him, "Promise before God to tell the truth. We know that this man is a sinner." 25 He replied, "I do not know whether he is a sinner. I do know one thing – that although I was blind, now I can see." 26 Then they said to him, "What did he do to you? How did he cause you to see?" 27 He answered, "I told you already and you didn't listen. Why do you want to hear it again? You people don't want to become his disciples too, do you?"

28 They heaped insults on him, saying, "You are his disciple! We are disciples of Moses! 29 We know that God has spoken to Moses! We do not know where this man comes from!" 30 The man replied, "This is a remarkable thing, that you don't know where he comes from, and yet he caused me to see! 31 We know that God doesn't listen to sinners, but if anyone is devout and does his will, God listens to him. 32 Never before has anyone heard of someone causing a man born blind to see. 33 If this man were not from God, he could do nothing." 34 They replied, "You were born completely in sinfulness, and yet you presume to teach us?" So they threw him out.

Jesus Identifies Himself to the Man
-Jerusalem-
John 9:35-38

35 Jesus heard that they had thrown him out, so he found the man and said to him, *"Do you believe in the Son of Man?"* 36 The man replied, "And who is he, sir, that I may believe in him?" 37 Jesus told him, *"You have seen him; he is the one speaking with you."* 38 He said, "Lord, I believe," and he worshiped him.

Spiritual Blindness of the Pharisees
-Jerusalem-
John 9:39-41

39 Jesus said, *"For judgment I have come into this world, so that those who do not see may gain their sight, and the ones who see may become blind."*

40 Some of the Pharisees who were with him heard this and asked him, "We are not blind too, are we?" 41 Jesus replied, *"If you were blind, you would not be guilty of sin, but now because you claim that you can see, your guilt remains."*

The Shepherd and His Flock
-Jerusalem-
John 10:1-18

1 "I tell you the solemn truth, the one who does not enter the sheepfold by the door, but climbs in some other way, is a thief and a robber. 2 The one who enters by the door is the shepherd of the sheep. 3 The doorkeeper opens the door for him, and the sheep hear his voice. He calls his own sheep by name and leads them out. 4 When he has brought all his own sheep out, he goes ahead of them, and the sheep follow him because they recognize his voice. 5 They will never follow a stranger, but will run away from him, because they do not recognize the stranger's voice." 6 Jesus told them this parable, but they did not understand what he was saying to them.

7 So Jesus said again, *"I tell you the solemn truth, I am the door for the sheep. 8 All who came before me were thieves and robbers, but the sheep did not listen to them. 9 I am the door. If anyone enters through me, he will be saved, and will come in and go out, and find pasture. 10 The thief comes only to steal and kill and destroy; I have come so that they may have life, and may have it abundantly.*

11 "I am the good shepherd. The good shepherd lays down his life for the sheep. 12 The hired hand, who is not a shepherd and does not own sheep, sees the wolf coming and abandons the sheep and runs away. So, the wolf attacks the sheep and scatters them. 13 Because he is a hired hand and is not concerned about the sheep, he runs away."

14 "I am the good shepherd. I know my own and my own know me – 15 just as the Father knows me and I know the Father – and I lay down my life for the sheep. 16 I have other sheep that do not come from this sheepfold. I must bring them too, and they will listen to my voice, so that there will be one flock and one shepherd. 17 This is why the Father loves me – because I lay down my life, so that I may take it back again. 18 No one takes it away from me, but I lay it down of my own free will. I have the authority to lay it down, and I have the authority to take it back again. This commandment I received from my Father."

The Unbelief of the Jews
-Jerusalem-
John 10:19-21

19 Another sharp division took place among the Jewish people because of these words. 20 Many of them were saying, "He is possessed by a demon and has lost his mind! Why do you listen to him?" 21 Others said, "These are not the words of someone possessed by a demon. A demon cannot cause the blind to see, can it?"

Another Attempt to Stone Jesus for Blasphemy
-Jerusalem in the Temple-

22 Then came the feast of the Dedication in Jerusalem. 23 It was winter, and Jesus was walking in the temple area in Solomon's Portico. 24 The Jewish leaders surrounded him and asked, "How long will you keep us in suspense? If you are the Christ, tell us plainly." 25 Jesus replied, *"I told you and you do not believe. The deeds I do in my Father's name testify about me. 26 But you refuse to believe because you are not my sheep. 27 My sheep listen to my voice, and I know them, and they follow me. 28 I give them eternal life, and they will never perish; no one will snatch them from my hand. 29 My Father, who has given them to me, is greater than all, and no one can snatch them from my Father's hand. 30 The Father and I are one."*

31 The Jewish leaders picked up rocks again to stone him to death. 32 Jesus said to them, *"I have shown you many good deeds from the Father. For which one of them are you going to stone me?"* 33 The Jewish leaders replied, "We are not going to stone you for a good deed but for blasphemy, because you, a man, are claiming to be God."

34 Jesus answered, *"Is it not written in your law, 'I said, you are gods'? 35 If those people to whom the word of God came were called 'gods' (and the scripture cannot be broken), 36 do you say about the one whom the Father set apart and sent into the world, 'You are blaspheming,' because I said, 'I am the Son of God'? 37 If I do not perform the deeds of my Father, do not believe me. 38 But if I do them, even if you do not believe me, believe the deeds, so that you may come to know and understand that I am in the Father and the Father is in me."* 39 Then they attempted again to seize him, but he escaped their clutches.

Jesus Goes from Jerusalem to Perea
John 10:40-42

40 Jesus went back across the Jordan River again to the place where John had been baptizing at an earlier time, and he stayed there. 41 Many came to him and began to say, "John performed no miraculous sign, but everything John said about this man was true!" 42 And many believed in Jesus there.

The Narrow Door
-Itineration toward Jerusalem while in Perea-
Luke 13:22-30

22 Then Jesus traveled throughout towns and villages, teaching and making his way toward Jerusalem. 23 Someone asked him, "Lord, will only a few be saved?" So, he said to them, *24 "Exert every effort to enter through the narrow door, because many, I tell you, will try to enter and will not be able to. 25 Once the head of the house gets up and shuts the door, then you will stand outside and start to knock on the door and beg him, 'Lord, let us in!' But he will answer you, 'I don't know where you come from.' 26 Then you will begin to say, 'We ate and drank in your presence, and you taught in our streets.' 27 But he will reply, 'I don't know where you come from! Go away from me, all you evildoers!' 28 There will be weeping and gnashing of teeth when you see Abraham, Isaac, Jacob, and all the prophets in the kingdom of God but you yourselves thrown out. 29 Then people will come from east and west, and from north and south, and take their places at the banquet table in the kingdom of God. 30 But indeed, some are last who will be first, and some are first who will be last."*

Jesus' Sorrow for Jerusalem
-Perea-
Luke 13:31-35

31 At that time, some Pharisees came up and said to Jesus, "Get away from here, because Herod wants to kill you." 32 But he said to them, *"Go and tell that fox, 'Look, I am casting out demons and performing healings today and tomorrow, and on the third day I will complete my work. 33 Nevertheless I must go on my way today and tomorrow and the next day, because it is impossible that a prophet should be killed outside Jerusalem.' 34 O Jerusalem, Jerusalem, you who kill the prophets and stone those who are sent to you! How often I have longed to gather your children together as a hen gathers her chicks under her wings, but you would have none of it! 35 Look, your house is forsaken! And I tell you, you will not see me until you say, 'Blessed is the one who comes in the name of the Lord!'"*

Jesus at a Pharisee's House
-Perea-
Luke 14:1-14

1 Now one Sabbath when Jesus went to dine at the house of a leader of the Pharisees, they were watching him closely. 2 There right in front of him was a man suffering from dropsy. 3 So Jesus

asked the experts in religious law and the Pharisees, *"Is it lawful to heal on the Sabbath or not?"* 4 But they remained silent. So Jesus took hold of the man, healed him, and sent him away. 5 Then he said to them, *"Which of you, if you have a son or an ox that has fallen into a well on a Sabbath day, will not immediately pull him out?"* 6 But they could not reply to this.

7 Then when Jesus noticed how the guests chose the places of honor, he told them a parable. He said to them, *8 "When you are invited by someone to a wedding feast, do not take the place of honor, because a person more distinguished than you may have been invited by your host. 9 So the host who invited both of you will come and say to you, 'Give this man your place.' Then, ashamed, you will begin to move to the least important place. 10 But when you are invited, go and take the least important place, so that when your host approaches he will say to you, 'Friend, move up here to a better place.' Then you will be honored in the presence of all who share the meal with you. 11 For everyone who exalts himself will be humbled, but the one who humbles himself will be exalted."*

12 He said also to the man who had invited him, *"When you host a dinner or a banquet, don't invite your friends or your brothers or your relatives or rich neighbors so you can be invited by them in return and get repaid. 13 But when you host an elaborate meal, invite the poor, the crippled, the lame, and the blind. 14 Then you will be blessed, because they cannot repay you, for you will be repaid at the resurrection of the righteous."*

The Parable of the Great Banquet
-Perea-
Luke 14:15-24

15 When one of those at the meal with Jesus heard this, he said to him, "Blessed is everyone who will feast in the kingdom of God!" 16 But Jesus said to him, *"A man once gave a great banquet and invited many guests. 17 At the time for the banquet he sent his slave to tell those who had been invited, 'Come, because everything is now ready.'"* 18 "But one after another they all began to make excuses. The first said to him, 'I have bought a field, and I must go out and see it. Please excuse me.'" 19 "Another said, 'I have bought five yoke of oxen, and I am going out to examine them. Please excuse me.'" 20 "Another said, 'I just got married, and I cannot come.'" 21 "So the slave came back and

reported this to his master. Then the master of the household was furious and said to his slave, 'Go out quickly to the streets and alleys of the city, and bring in the poor, the crippled, the blind, and the lame.'" 22 "Then the slave said, 'Sir, what you instructed has been done, and there is still room.'" 23 "So the master said to his slave, 'Go out to the highways and country roads and urge people to come in, so that my house will be filled. 24 For I tell you, not one of those individuals who were invited will taste my banquet!'"

The Cost of Being a Disciple
-Perea-
Luke 14:25-35

25 Now large crowds were accompanying Jesus, and turning to them he said, 26 *"If anyone comes to me and does not hate his own father and mother, and wife and children, and brothers and sisters, and even his own life, he cannot be my disciple. 27 Whoever does not carry his own cross and follow me cannot be my disciple." 28 "For which of you, wanting to build a tower, doesn't sit down first and compute the cost to see if he has enough money to complete it? 29 Otherwise, when he has laid a foundation and is not able to finish the tower, all who see it will begin to make fun of him. 30 They will say, 'This man began to build and was not able to finish!'" 31 "Or what king, going out to confront another king in battle, will not sit down first and determine whether he is able with ten thousand to oppose the one coming against him with twenty thousand? 32 If he cannot succeed, he will send a representative while the other is still a long way off and ask for terms of peace. 33 In the same way therefore not one of you can be my disciple if he does not renounce all his own possessions."*

34 *"Salt is good, but if salt loses its flavor, how can its flavor be restored? 35 It is of no value for the soil or for the manure pile; it is to be thrown out. The one who has ears to hear had better listen!"*

The Parable of the Lost Sheep
-Perea-
Luke 15:1-7

1 Now all the tax collectors and sinners were coming to hear him. 2 But the Pharisees and the experts in the law were complaining, "This man welcomes sinners and eats with them."

3 So Jesus told them this parable: *4 "Which one of you, if he has a hundred sheep and loses one of them, would not leave the ninety-nine in the open pasture and go look for the one that is lost until he finds it? 5 Then when he has found it, he places it on his shoulders, rejoicing. 6 Returning home, he calls together his friends and neighbors, telling them, 'Rejoice with me, because I have found my sheep that was lost.' 7 I tell you, in the same way there will be more joy in heaven over one sinner who repents than over ninety-nine righteous people who have no need to repent."*

The Parable of the Lost Coin
-Perea-
Luke 15:8-10

8 "Or what woman, if she has ten silver coins and loses one of them, does not light a lamp, sweep the house, and search thoroughly until she finds it? 9 Then when she has found it, she calls together her friends and neighbors, saying, 'Rejoice with me, for I have found the coin that I had lost.' 10 In the same way, I tell you, there is joy in the presence of God's angels over one sinner who repents."

The Parable of the Lost Son
-Perea-
Luke 15:11-32

11 Then Jesus said, *"A man had two sons. 12 The younger of them said to his father, 'Father, give me the share of the estate that will belong to me.' So, he divided his assets between them."* 13 *"After a few days, the younger son gathered together all he had and left on a journey to a distant country, and there he squandered his wealth with a wild lifestyle. 14 Then after he had spent everything, a severe famine took place in that country, and he began to be in need. 15 So he went and worked for one of the citizens of that country, who sent him to his fields to feed pigs. 16 He was longing to eat the carob pods the pigs were eating, but no one gave him anything."* 17 *"But when he came to his senses he said, 'How many of my father's hired workers have food enough to spare, but here I am dying from hunger! 18 I will get up and go to my father and say to him, "Father, I have sinned against heaven and against you. 19 I am no longer worthy to be called your son; treat me like one of your hired workers."' 20 So he got up and went to his father."* *"But while he was still a long way from*

home his father saw him, and his heart went out to him; he ran and hugged his son and kissed him." 21 "Then his son said to him, 'Father, I have sinned against heaven and against you; I am no longer worthy to be called your son.' 22 But the father said to his slaves, 'Hurry! Bring the best robe, and put it on him! Put a ring on his finger and sandals on his feet! 23 Bring the fattened calf and kill it! Let us eat and celebrate 24 because this son of mine was dead, and is alive again – he was lost and is found!' So, they began to celebrate."

25 "Now his older son was in the field. As he came and approached the house, he heard music and dancing. 26 So he called one of the slaves and asked what was happening. 27 The slave replied, 'Your brother has returned, and your father has killed the fattened calf because he got his son back safe and sound.'" 28 "But the older son became angry and refused to go in. His father came out and appealed to him, 29 but he answered his father, 'Look! These many years I have worked like a slave for you, and I never disobeyed your commands. Yet you never gave me even a goat so that I could celebrate with my friends! 30 But when this son of yours came back, who has devoured your assets with prostitutes; you killed the fattened calf for him!'" 31 "Then the father said to him, 'Son, you are always with me, and everything that belongs to me is yours. 32 It was appropriate to celebrate and be glad, for your brother was dead, and is alive; he was lost and is found.'"

The Parable of the Shrewd Manager
-Perea-
Luke 16:1-13

1 Jesus also said to the disciples, *"There was a rich man who was informed of accusations that his manager was wasting his assets. 2 So he called the manager in and said to him, 'What is this I hear about you? Turn in the account of your administration, because you can no longer be my manager.'" 3 "Then the manager said to himself, 'What should I do, since my master is taking my position away from me? I'm not strong enough to dig, and I'm too ashamed to beg. 4 I know what to do so that when I am put out of management, people will welcome me into their homes.'" 5 "So he contacted his master's debtors one by one. He asked the first, 'How much do you owe my master?'" 6 "The man replied, 'A hundred measures of olive oil.'" "The manager said to*

him, 'Take your bill, sit down quickly, and write fifty.'" 7 "Then he said to another, 'and how much do you owe?'" "The second man replied, 'A hundred measures of wheat.'" "The manager said to him, 'Take your bill, and write eighty.'" 8 "The master commended the dishonest manager because he acted shrewdly. For the people of this world are more shrewd in dealing with their contemporaries than the people of light. 9 And I tell you, make friends for yourselves by how you use worldly wealth, so that when it runs out you will be welcomed into the eternal homes."

10 "The one who is faithful in a very little is also faithful in much, and the one who is dishonest in a very little is also dishonest in much. 11 If then you haven't been trustworthy in handling worldly wealth, who will entrust you with the true riches? 12 And if you haven't been trustworthy with someone else's property, who will give you your own?" 13 "No servant can serve two masters, for either he will hate the one and love the other, or he will be devoted to the one and despise the other. You cannot serve God and money."

The Pharisees Reproved
-Perea-
Luke 16: 14-18

14 The Pharisees (who loved money) heard all this and ridiculed him. 15 But Jesus said to them, *"You are the ones who justify yourselves in men's eyes, but God knows your hearts. For what is highly prized among men is utterly detestable in God's sight."*

16 "The law and the prophets were in force until John; since then, the good news of the kingdom of God has been proclaimed, and everyone is urged to enter it. 17 But it is easier for heaven and earth to pass away than for one tiny stroke of a letter in the law to become void."

18 "Everyone who divorces his wife and marries someone else commits adultery, and the one who marries a woman divorced from her husband commits adultery."

The Rich Man and Lazarus
-Perea-
Luke 16:19-31

19 "There was a rich man who dressed in purple and fine linen and who feasted sumptuously every day. 20 But at his gate lay a poor man named Lazarus whose body was covered with sores, 21 who longed to eat what fell from the rich man's table. In addition, the dogs came and licked his sores."

22 "Now the poor man died and was carried by the angels to Abraham's side. The rich man also died and was buried. 23 And in hell, as he was in torment, he looked up and saw Abraham far off with Lazarus at his side. 24 So he called out, 'Father Abraham, have mercy on me, and send Lazarus to dip the tip of his finger in water and cool my tongue, because I am in anguish in this fire.'"
25 "But Abraham said, 'Child, remember that in your lifetime you received your good things and Lazarus likewise bad things, but now he is comforted here and you are in anguish. 26 Besides all this, a great chasm has been fixed between us, so that those who want to cross over from here to you cannot do so, and no one can cross from there to us.'" 27 "So the rich man said, 'Then I beg you, father – send Lazarus to my father's house 28 (for I have five brothers) to warn them so that they don't come into this place of torment.'" 29 "But Abraham said, 'They have Moses and the prophets; they must respond to them.'" 30 "Then the rich man said, 'No, father Abraham, but if someone from the dead goes to them, they will repent.'" 31 "He replied to him, 'If they do not respond to Moses and the prophets, they will not be convinced even if someone rises from the dead.'"

Sin, Faith and Duty
-Perea-
Luke 17:1-10

1 Jesus said to his disciples, *"Stumbling blocks are sure to come, but woe to the one through whom they come! 2 It would be better for him to have a millstone tied around his neck and be thrown into the sea than for him to cause one of these little ones to sin. 3 Watch yourselves!" "If your brother sins, rebuke him. If he repents, forgive him. 4 Even if he sins against you seven times in a day, and seven times returns to you saying, 'I repent,' you must forgive him."*

5 The apostles said to the Lord, "Increase our faith!" 6 So the Lord replied, *"If you had faith the size of a mustard seed, you could say to this black mulberry tree, 'Be pulled out by the roots and planted in the sea,' and it would obey you."*

7 "Would any one of you say to your slave, who comes in from the field after plowing or shepherding sheep, 'Come at once and sit down for a meal'? 8 Won't the master instead say to him, 'Get my dinner ready, and make yourself ready to serve me while I eat and drink. Then you may eat and drink'? 9 He won't thank the slave because he did what he was told, will he? 10 So you too, when you have done everything you were commanded to do, should say, 'We are slaves undeserving of special praise; we have only done what was our duty.'"

Sickness and Death of Lazarus
-From Perea to Bethany near Jerusalem-
John 11:1-16

1 Now a certain man named Lazarus was sick. He was from Bethany, the village where Mary and her sister Martha lived. 2 (Now it was Mary who anointed the Lord with perfumed oil and wiped his feet dry with her hair, whose brother Lazarus was sick.) 3 So the sisters sent a message to Jesus, "Lord, look, the one you love is sick." 4 When Jesus heard this, he said, *"This sickness will not lead to death, but to God's glory, so that the Son of God may be glorified through it."* 5 (Now Jesus loved Martha and her sister and Lazarus.)

6 So when he heard that Lazarus was sick, he remained in the place where he was for two more days. 7 Then after this, he said to his disciples, *"Let us go to Judea again."* 8 The disciples replied, "Rabbi, the Jewish leaders were just now trying to stone you to death! Are you going there again?" 9 Jesus replied, *"Are there not twelve hours in a day? If anyone walks around in the daytime, he does not stumble, because he sees the light of this world. 10 But if anyone walks around at night, he stumbles, because the light is not in him."*

11 After he said this, he added, *"Our friend Lazarus has fallen asleep. But I am going there to awaken him."* 12 Then the disciples replied, "Lord, if he has fallen asleep, he will recover." 13 (Now Jesus had been talking about his death, but they thought he had been talking about real sleep.)

14 Then Jesus told them plainly, *"Lazarus has died, 15 and I am glad for your sake that I was not there, so that you may believe. But let us go to him."* 16 So Thomas (called Didymus) said to his fellow disciples, "Let us go too, so that we may die with him."

Jesus Comforts the Sisters
-Bethany near Jerusalem-
John 11:17-37

17 When Jesus arrived, he found that Lazarus had been in the tomb four days already. 18 (Now Bethany was less than two miles from Jerusalem, 19 so many of the Jewish people of the region had come to Martha and Mary to console them over the loss of their brother.) 20 So when Martha heard that Jesus was coming, she went out to meet him, but Mary was sitting in the house. 21 Martha said to Jesus, "Lord, if you had been here, my brother would not have died. 22 But even now I know that whatever you ask from God, God will grant you."

23 Jesus replied, *"Your brother will come back to life again."* 24 Martha said, "I know that he will come back to life again in the resurrection at the last day." 25 Jesus said to her, *"I am the resurrection and the life. The one who believes in me will live even if he dies, 26 and the one who lives and believes in me will never die. Do you believe this?"* 27 She replied, "Yes, Lord, I believe that you are the Christ, the Son of God who comes into the world."

28 And when she had said this, Martha went and called her sister Mary, saying privately, "The Teacher is here and is asking for you." 29 So when Mary heard this, she got up quickly and went to him. 30 (Now Jesus had not yet entered the village, but was still in the place where Martha had come out to meet him.) 31 Then the people who were with Mary in the house consoling her saw her get up quickly and go out. They followed her, because they thought she was going to the tomb to weep there.

32 Now when Mary came to the place where Jesus was and saw him, she fell at his feet and said to him, "Lord, if you had been here, my brother would not have died." 33 When Jesus saw her weeping, and the people who had come with her weeping, he was intensely moved in spirit and greatly distressed. 34 He asked, *"Where have you laid him?"* They replied, "Lord, come and see." 35 Jesus wept. 36 Then the people who had come to mourn said, "Look how much he loved him!" 37 But some of them said, "This is the man who caused the blind man to see! Couldn't he have done something to keep Lazarus from dying?"

Jesus Raises Lazarus from the Dead
-Bethany near Jerusalem-
John 11:38-44

38 Jesus, intensely moved again, came to the tomb. (Now it was a cave, and a stone was placed across it.) 39 Jesus said, *"Take away the stone."* Martha, the sister of the deceased, replied, "Lord,

by this time the body will have a bad smell, because he has been buried four days." 40 Jesus responded, *"Didn't I tell you that if you believe, you would see the glory of God?" 41 So they took away the stone. Jesus looked upward and said, "Father, I thank you that you have listened to me. 42 I knew that you always listen to me, but I said this for the sake of the crowd standing around here, that they may believe that you sent me."* 43 When he had said this, he shouted in a loud voice, "Lazarus, come out!" 44 The one who had died came out, his feet and hands tied up with strips of cloth, and a cloth wrapped around his face. Jesus said to them, *"Unwrap him and let him go."*

The Plot to Kill Jesus
-Jerusalem and Ephraim near the Wilderness-
John 11:45-54

45 Then many of the people, who had come with Mary and had seen the things Jesus did, believed in him. 46 But some of them went to the Pharisees and reported to them what Jesus had done. 47 So the chief priests and the Pharisees called the council together and said, "What are we doing? For this man is performing many miraculous signs. 48 If we allow him to go on in this way, everyone will believe in him, and the Romans will come and take away our sanctuary and our nation."

49 Then one of them, Caiaphas, who was high priest that year, said, "You know nothing at all! 50 You do not realize that it is more to your advantage to have one man die for the people than for the whole nation to perish." 51 (Now he did not say this on his own, but because he was high priest that year, he prophesied that Jesus was going to die for the Jewish nation, 52 and not for the Jewish nation only, but to gather together into one the children of God who are scattered.) 53 So from that day they planned together to kill him.

54 Therefore Jesus no longer went around publicly among the Judeans, but went away from there to the region near the wilderness, to a town called Ephraim, and stayed there with his disciples.

Ten Healed of Leprosy
-Passing through Samaria and Galilee-
Luke 17:11-19

11 Now on the way to Jerusalem, Jesus was passing along between Samaria and Galilee. 12 As he was entering a village, ten men with leprosy met him. They stood at a distance, 13 raised their voices and said, "Jesus, Master, have mercy on us." 14 When he saw them he said, *"Go and show yourselves to the priests."* And as they went along, they were cleansed. 15 Then one of them, when he saw he was healed, turned back, praising God with a loud voice. 16 He fell with his face to the ground at Jesus' feet and thanked him. (Now he was a Samaritan.) 17 Then Jesus said, *"Were not ten cleansed? Where are the other nine? 18 Was no one found to turn back and give praise to God except this foreigner?"* 19 Then he said to the man, *"Get up and go your way. Your faith has made you well."*

The Coming of the Kingdom of God
-Samaria or Galilee-
Luke 17:20-37

20 Now at one point the Pharisees asked Jesus when the kingdom of God was coming, so he answered, *"The kingdom of God is not coming with signs to be observed, 21 nor will they say, 'Look, here it is!' or 'There!' For indeed, the kingdom of God is in your midst."*

22 Then he said to the disciples, *"The days are coming when you will desire to see one of the days of the Son of Man, and you will not see it. 23 Then people will say to you, 'Look, there he is!' or 'Look, here he is!' Do not go out or chase after them. 24 For just like the lightning flashes and lights up the sky from one side to the other, so will the Son of Man be in his day. 25 But first he must suffer many things and be rejected by this generation." 26 "Just as it was in the days of Noah, so too it will be in the days of the Son of Man. 27 People were eating, they were drinking, they were marrying, they were being given in marriage – right up to the day Noah entered the ark. Then the flood came and destroyed them all." 28 "Likewise, just as it was in the days of Lot, people were eating, drinking, buying, selling, planting, building; 29 but on the day Lot went out from Sodom, fire and sulfur rained down from heaven and destroyed them all." 30 "It will be the same on the day the Son of Man is revealed. 31 On that day, anyone who is on the roof, with his goods in the house, must not come down to take them away, and likewise the person in the field must not turn back. 32 Remember Lot's wife! 33 Whoever tries to keep his life will*

lose it, but whoever loses his life will preserve it. *34 I tell you, in that night there will be two people in one bed; one will be taken and the other left. 35 There will be two women grinding grain together; one will be taken and the other left."*

37 Then the disciples said to him, "Where, Lord?" He replied to them, *"Where the dead body is, there the vultures will gather."*

The Parable of the Persistent Widow
-Itineration toward Jerusalem-
Luke 18:1-8

1 Then Jesus told them a parable to show them they should always pray and not lose heart. 2 He said, *"In a certain city there was a judge who neither feared God nor respected people. 3 There was also a widow in that city who kept coming to him and saying, 'Give me justice against my adversary.' 4 For a while he refused, but later on he said to himself, 'Though I neither fear God nor have regard for people, 5 yet because this widow keeps on bothering me, I will give her justice, or in the end she will wear me out by her unending pleas.'"* 6 And the Lord said, *"Listen to what the unrighteous judge says! 7 Won't God give justice to his chosen ones, who cry out to him day and night? Will he delay long to help them? 8 I tell you, he will give them justice speedily. Nevertheless, when the Son of Man comes, will he find faith on earth?"*

The Parable of the Pharisee and the Tax Collector
-Itineration toward Jerusalem-
Luke 18:9-14

9 Jesus also told this parable to some who were confident that they were righteous and looked down on everyone else. *10 "Two men went up to the temple to pray, one a Pharisee and the other a tax collector. 11 The Pharisee stood and prayed about himself like this: 'God, I thank you that I am not like other people: extortionists, unrighteous people, adulterers – or even like this tax collector. 12 I fast twice a week; I give a tenth of everything I get.'" 13 "The tax collector, however, stood far off and would not even look up to heaven, but beat his breast and said, 'God, be merciful to me, sinner that I am!'" 14 "I tell you that this man went down to his home justified rather than the Pharisee. For everyone who exalts himself will be humbled, but he who humbles himself will be exalted."*

Precepts Respecting Divorce
-Perea-
Matthew 19:1-12

1 Now when Jesus finished these sayings, he left Galilee and went to the region of Judea beyond the Jordan River. 2 Large crowds followed him, and he healed them there.

3 Then some Pharisees came to him in order to test him. They asked, "Is it lawful to divorce a wife for any cause?" 4 He answered, *"Have you not read that from the beginning the Creator made them male and female, 5 and said, 'For this reason a man will leave his father and mother and will be united with his wife, and the two will become one flesh'? 6 So they are no longer two, but one flesh. Therefore, what God has joined together, let no one separate."* 7 They said to him, "Why then did Moses command us to give a certificate of dismissal and to divorce her?" 8 Jesus said to them, *"Moses permitted you to divorce your wives because of your hard hearts, but from the beginning it was not this way. 9 Now I say to you that whoever divorces his wife, except for immorality, and marries another woman commits adultery."* 10 The disciples said to him, *"If this is the case of a husband with a wife, it is better not to marry!"* 11 He said to them, *"Not everyone can accept this statement, except those to whom it has been given. 12 For there are some eunuchs who were that way from birth, and some who were made eunuchs by others, and some who became eunuchs for the sake of the kingdom of heaven. The one who is able to accept this should accept it."*

The Little Children and Jesus
-Perea-
Mark 10:13-16

13 Now people were bringing little children to him for him to touch, but the disciples scolded those who brought them. 14 But when Jesus saw this, he was indignant and said to them, *"Let the little children come to me and do not try to stop them, for the kingdom of God belongs to such as these. 15 I tell you the truth, whoever does not receive the kingdom of God like a child will never enter it."* 16 After he took the children in his arms, he placed his hands on them and blessed them.

The Rich Young Man

Matthew 19:16-19

16 Now someone came up to him and said, "Teacher, what good thing must I do to gain eternal life?" 17 He said to him, *"Why do you ask me about what is good? There is only one who is good. But if you want to enter into life, keep the commandments."* 18 "Which ones?" he asked. Jesus replied, *"Do not murder, do not commit adultery, do not steal, do not give false testimony, 19 honor your father and mother, and love your neighbor as yourself."*

Mark 10:20-25

20 The man said to him, "Teacher, I have wholeheartedly obeyed all these laws since my youth." 21 As Jesus looked at him, he felt love for him and said, *"You lack one thing. Go, sell whatever you have and give the money to the poor, and you will have treasure in heaven. Then come, follow me."* 22 But at this statement, the man looked sad and went away sorrowful, for he was very rich.

23 Then Jesus looked around and said to his disciples, *"How hard it is for the rich to enter the kingdom of God!"* 24 The disciples were astonished at these words. But again, Jesus said to them, *"Children, how hard it is to enter the kingdom of God! 25 It is easier for a camel to go through the eye of a needle than for a rich person to enter the kingdom of God."*

Matthew 19:25-28

25 The disciples were greatly astonished when they heard this and said, "Then who can be saved?" 26 Jesus looked at them and replied, *"This is impossible for mere humans, but for God all things are possible."* 27 Then Peter said to him, "Look, we have left everything to follow you! What then will there be for us?" 28 Jesus said to them, *"I tell you the truth: In the age when all things are renewed, when the Son of Man sits on his glorious throne, you who have followed me will also sit on twelve thrones, judging the twelve tribes of Israel."*

Mark 10:29-31

29 Jesus said, *"I tell you the truth, there is no one who has left home or brothers or sisters or mother or father or children or fields for my sake and for the sake of the gospel 30 who will not receive in this age a hundred times as much – homes, brothers, sisters, mothers, children, fields, all with persecutions – and in the*

age to come, eternal life. *31 But many who are first will be last, and the last first."*

The Parable of the Workers in the Vineyard
-Perea-
Matthew 20:1-16

1 "For the kingdom of heaven is like a landowner who went out early in the morning to hire workers for his vineyard. 2 And after agreeing with the workers for the standard wage, he sent them into his vineyard." 3 "When it was about nine o'clock in the morning, he went out again and saw others standing around in the marketplace without work. 4 He said to them, 'You go into the vineyard too, and I will give you whatever is right.' 5 So they went." "When he went out again about noon and three o'clock that afternoon, he did the same thing. 6 And about five o'clock that afternoon he went out and found others standing around, and said to them, 'Why are you standing here all day without work?'" 7 "They said to him, 'Because no one hired us.'" "He said to them, 'You go and work in the vineyard too.'" 8 "When it was evening the owner of the vineyard said to his manager, 'Call the workers and give the pay starting with the last hired until the first.'" 9 "When those hired about five o'clock came, each received a full day's pay. 10 And when those hired first came, they thought they would receive more. But each one also received the standard wage. 11 When they received it, they began to complain against the landowner, 12 saying, 'These last fellows worked one hour, and you have made them equal to us who bore the hardship and burning heat of the day.'" 13 "And the landowner replied to one of them, 'Friend, I am not treating you unfairly. Didn't you agree with me to work for the standard wage? 14 Take what is yours and go. I want to give to this last man the same as I gave to you. 15 Am I not permitted to do what I want with what belongs to me? Or are you envious because I am generous?'"

16 "So the last will be first, and the first last."

Jesus Again Predicts His Death
-On the road up to Jerusalem-
Matthew 20:17-19

17 As Jesus was going up to Jerusalem, he took the twelve aside privately and said to them on the way, *18 "Look, we are going up to Jerusalem, and the Son of Man will be handed over to the chief*

priests and the experts in the law. They will condemn him to death, 19 and will turn him over to the Gentiles to be mocked and flogged severely and crucified. Yet on the third day, he will be raised."

Luke 18:34

34 But the twelve understood none of these things. This saying was hidden from them, and they did not grasp what Jesus meant.

Warning against Ambitious Pride
-On the road up to Jerusalem-
Matthew 20:20-21

20 Then the mother of the sons of Zebedee came to him with her sons, and kneeling down she asked him for a favor. 21 He said to her, *"What do you want?"* She replied, "Permit these two sons of mine to sit, one at your right hand and one at your left, in your kingdom."

Mark 10:38-45

38 But Jesus said to them, *"You don't know what you are asking! Are you able to drink the cup I drink or be baptized with the baptism I experience?"* 39 They said to him, "We are able." Then Jesus said to them, *"You will drink the cup I drink, and you will be baptized with the baptism I experience, 40 but to sit at my right or at my left is not mine to give. It is for those for whom it has been prepared."*

41 Now when the other ten heard this, they became angry with James and John. 42 Jesus called them and said to them, *"You know that those who are recognized as rulers of the Gentiles lord it over them, and those in high positions use their authority over them. 43 But it is not this way among you. Instead whoever wants to be great among you must be your servant, 44 and whoever wants to be first among you must be the slave of all. 45 For even the Son of Man did not come to be served but to serve, and to give his life as a ransom for many."*

Blind Bartimaeus Receives His Sight
-Old Jericho to New Jericho-
See Note: Jericho
Mark 10:46-51

46 They came to Jericho. As Jesus and his disciples and a large crowd were leaving Jericho, Bartimaeus the son of Timaeus, a blind beggar, was sitting by the road. 47 When he heard that it was Jesus the Nazarene, he began to shout, "Jesus, Son of David, have

mercy on me!" 48 Many scolded him to get him to be quiet, but he shouted all the more, "Son of David, have mercy on me!" 49 Jesus stopped and said, *"Call him."* So they called the blind man and said to him, "Have courage! Get up! He is calling you." 50 He threw off his cloak, jumped up, and came to Jesus. 51 Then Jesus said to him, *"What do you want me to do for you?"* The blind man replied, "Rabbi, let me see again."

Luke 18:42-43

42 Jesus said to him, *"Receive your sight; your faith has healed you."* 43 And immediately he regained his sight and followed Jesus, praising God. When all the people saw it, they too gave praise to God.

Zacchaeus the Tax Collector
-Jericho-
Luke 19:1-10

1 Jesus entered Jericho and was passing through it. 2 Now a man named Zacchaeus was there; he was a chief tax collector and was rich. 3 He was trying to get a look at Jesus, but being a short man he could not see over the crowd. 4 So he ran on ahead and climbed up into a sycamore tree to see him, because Jesus was going to pass that way. 5 And when Jesus came to that place, he looked up and said to him, *"Zacchaeus, come down quickly, because I must stay at your house today."* 6 So he came down quickly and welcomed Jesus joyfully. 7 And when the people saw it, they all complained, "He has gone in to be the guest of a man who is a sinner." 8 But Zacchaeus stopped and said to the Lord, "Look, Lord, half of my possessions I now give to the poor, and if I have cheated anyone of anything, I am paying back four times as much!" 9 Then Jesus said to him, *"Today salvation has come to this household, because he too is a son of Abraham! 10 For the Son of Man came to seek and to save the lost."*

Two Blind Men Receive Sight
-Leaving Jericho-
Matthew 20:29-34

29 As they were leaving Jericho, a large crowd followed them. 30 Two blind men were sitting by the road. When they heard that Jesus was passing by, they shouted, "Have mercy on us, Lord, Son of David!" 31 The crowd scolded them to get them to be quiet. But they shouted even more loudly, "Lord, have mercy on us, Son

of David!" 32 Jesus stopped, called them, and said, *"What do you want me to do for you?"* 33 They said to him, "Lord, let our eyes be opened." 34 Moved with compassion, Jesus touched their eyes. Immediately they received their sight and followed him.

The Parable of the Ten Minas
-Jericho and the final ascent to Jerusalem-
Luke 19:11-28

11 While the people were listening to these things, Jesus proceeded to tell a parable, because he was near to Jerusalem, and because they thought that the kingdom of God was going to appear immediately. 12 Therefore he said, *"A nobleman went to a distant country to receive for himself a kingdom and then return. 13 And he summoned ten of his slaves, gave them ten minas, and said to them, 'Do business with these until I come back.'" 14 "But his citizens hated him and sent a delegation after him, saying, 'We do not want this man to be king over us!'" 15 "When he returned after receiving the kingdom, he summoned these slaves to whom he had given the money. He wanted to know how much they had earned by trading." 16 "So the first one came before him and said, 'Sir, your mina has made ten minas more.'" 17 "And the king said to him, 'Well done, good slave! Because you have been faithful in a very small matter, you will have authority over ten cities.'" 18 "Then the second one came and said, 'Sir, your mina has made five minas.'" 19 "So the king said to him, 'And you are to be over five cities.'" 20 "Then another slave came and said, 'Sir, here is your mina that I put away for safekeeping in a piece of cloth. 21 For I was afraid of you, because you are a severe man. You withdraw what you did not deposit and reap what you did not sow.'" 22 "The king said to him, 'I will judge you by your own words, you wicked slave! So, you knew, did you, that I was a severe man, withdrawing what I didn't deposit and reaping what I didn't sow? 23 Why then didn't you put my money in the bank, so that when I returned I could have collected it with interest?' 24 And he said to his attendants, 'Take the mina from him, and give it to the one who has ten.'" 25 "But they said to him, 'Sir, he has ten minas already!'"*

26 "'I tell you that everyone who has will be given more, but from the one who does not have, even what he has will be taken away. 27 But as for these enemies of mine who did not want me to be their king, bring them here and slaughter them in front of me!'"

28 After Jesus had said this, he continued on ahead, going up to Jerusalem.

Arrival at Bethany
-Bethany near Jerusalem-
John 11:55-57

55 Now the Jewish feast of Passover was near, and many people went up to Jerusalem from the rural areas before the Passover to cleanse themselves ritually. 56 Thus they were looking for Jesus, and saying to one another as they stood in the temple courts, "What do you think? That he won't come to the feast?" 57 (Now the chief priests and the Pharisees had given orders that anyone who knew where Jesus was should report it, so that they could arrest him.)

Jesus Anointed at Bethany
-Bethany-
See Note: Jesus Anointed
John 12:1-11

1 Then, six days before the Passover, Jesus came to Bethany, where Lazarus lived, whom he had raised from the dead. 2 So they prepared a dinner for Jesus there. Martha was serving, and Lazarus was among those present at the table with him. 3 Then Mary took three quarters of a pound of expensive aromatic oil from pure nard and anointed the feet of Jesus. She then wiped his feet dry with her hair. (Now the house was filled with the fragrance of the perfumed oil.) 4 But Judas Iscariot, one of his disciples (the one who was going to betray him) said, 5 "Why wasn't this oil sold for three hundred silver coins and the money given to the poor?" 6 (Now Judas said this not because he was concerned about the poor, but because he was a thief. As keeper of the money box, he used to steal what was put into it.) 7 So Jesus said, *"Leave her alone. She has kept it for the day of my burial. 8 For you will always have the poor with you, but you will not always have me!"*

9 Now a large crowd of Judeans learned that Jesus was there, and so they came not only because of him but also to see Lazarus whom he had raised from the dead. 10 So the chief priests planned to kill Lazarus too, 11 for on account of him many of the Jewish people from Jerusalem were going away and believing in Jesus.

The Triumphal Entry

Matthew 21:1-8

1 Now when they approached Jerusalem and came to Bethphage, at the Mount of Olives, Jesus sent two disciples, 2 telling them, *"Go to the village ahead of you. Right away you will find a donkey tied there, and a colt with her. Untie them and bring them to me. 3 If anyone says anything to you, you are to say, 'The Lord needs them,' and he will send them at once."* 4 This took place to fulfill what was spoken by the prophet: 5 "Tell the people of Zion, 'Look, your king is coming to you, unassuming and seated on a donkey, and on a colt, the foal of a donkey.'"

6 So the disciples went and did as Jesus had instructed them. 7 They brought the donkey and the colt and placed their cloaks on them, and he sat on them. 8 A very large crowd spread their cloaks on the road. Others cut branches from the trees and spread them on the road.

Luke 19:37-38

37 As he approached the road leading down from the Mount of Olives, the whole crowd of his disciples began to rejoice and praise God with a loud voice for all the mighty works they had seen: 38 "Blessed is the king who comes in the name of the Lord! Peace in heaven and glory in the highest!"

John 12:16-19

16 (His disciples did not understand these things when they first happened, but when Jesus was glorified, then they remembered that these things were written about him and that these things had happened to him.)

17 So the crowd who had been with him when he called Lazarus out of the tomb and raised him from the dead were continuing to testify about it. 18 Because they had heard that Jesus had performed this miraculous sign, the crowd went out to meet him. 19 Thus the Pharisees said to one another, "You see that you can do nothing. Look, the world has run off after him!"

Luke 19:39-44

39 But some of the Pharisees in the crowd said to him, "Teacher, rebuke your disciples." 40 He answered, *"I tell you, if they keep silent, the very stones will cry out!"*

41 Now when Jesus approached and saw the city, he wept over it, 42 saying, *"If you had only known on this day, even you, the things that make for peace! But now they are hidden from your*

eyes. 43 For the days will come upon you when your enemies will build an embankment against you and surround you and close in on you from every side. 44 They will demolish you – you and your children within your walls – and they will not leave within you one stone on top of another, because you did not recognize the time of your visitation from God."

Matthew 21:10-11

10 As he entered Jerusalem the whole city was thrown into an uproar, saying, "Who is this?" 11 And the crowds were saying, "This is the prophet Jesus, from Nazareth in Galilee."

Mark 11:11

11 Then Jesus entered Jerusalem and went to the temple. And after looking around at everything, he went out to Bethany with the twelve since it was already late.

Jesus Curses the Fig Tree
-From Bethany back to Jerusalem-
Mark 11:12-14

12 Now the next day, as they went out from Bethany, he was hungry. 13 After noticing in the distance a fig tree with leaves, he went to see if he could find any fruit on it. When he came to it he found nothing but leaves, for it was not the season for figs. 14 He said to it, *"May no one ever eat fruit from you again."* And his disciples heard it.

Second Cleansing of the Temple
-Jerusalem, in the Temple-
Mark 11:15-17

15 Then they came to Jerusalem. Jesus entered the temple area and began to drive out those who were selling and buying in the temple courts. He turned over the tables of the money changers and the chairs of those selling doves, 16 and he would not permit anyone to carry merchandise through the temple courts. 17 Then he began to teach them and said, *"Is it not written: 'My house will be called a house of prayer for all nations'? But you have turned it into a den of robbers!"*

Jesus Teaches and Heals at the Temple
-Jerusalem at the Temple-
Matthew 21:14-17

14 The blind and lame came to him in the temple courts, and he healed them. 15 But when the chief priests and the experts in the law saw the wonderful things he did and heard the children crying out in the temple courts, "Hosanna to the Son of David," they became indignant 16 and said to him, "Do you hear what they are saying?" Jesus said to them, *"Yes. Have you never read, 'Out of the mouths of children and nursing infants you have prepared praise for yourself'?"* 17 And leaving them, he went out of the city to Bethany and spent the night there.

Luke 19:47-48

47 Jesus was teaching daily in the temple courts. The chief priests and the experts in the law and the prominent leaders among the people were seeking to assassinate him, 48 but they could not find a way to do it, for all the people hung on his words.

Jesus Predicts His Death
-Jerusalem-
John 12:20-36

20 Now some Greeks were among those who had gone up to worship at the feast. 21 So these approached Philip, who was from Bethsaida in Galilee, and requested, "Sir, we would like to see Jesus." 22 Philip went and told Andrew, and they both went and told Jesus. 23 Jesus replied, *"The time has come for the Son of Man to be glorified. 24 I tell you the solemn truth, unless a kernel of wheat falls into the ground and dies, it remains by itself alone. But if it dies, it produces much grain. 25 The one who loves his life destroys it, and the one who hates his life in this world guards it for eternal life. 26 If anyone wants to serve me, he must follow me, and where I am, my servant will be too. If anyone serves me, the Father will honor him."*

27 "Now my soul is greatly distressed. And what should I say? 'Father, deliver me from this hour'? No, but for this very reason I have come to this hour. 28 Father, glorify your name." Then a voice came from heaven, "I have glorified it, and I will glorify it again." 29 The crowd that stood there and heard the voice said that it had thundered. Others said that an angel had spoken to him. 30 Jesus said, *"This voice has not come for my benefit but for yours. 31 Now is the judgment of this world; now the ruler of this world will be driven out. 32 And I, when I am lifted up from the earth, will draw all people to myself."* 33 (Now he said this to indicate clearly what kind of death he was going to die.)

34 Then the crowd responded, *"We have heard from the law that the Christ will remain forever. How can you say, 'The Son of Man must be lifted up'? Who is this Son of Man?"* 35 Jesus replied, *"The light is with you for a little while longer. Walk while you have the light, so that the darkness may not overtake you. The one who walks in the darkness does not know where he is going. 36 While you have the light, believe in the light, so that you may become sons of light."* When Jesus had said these things, he went away and hid himself from them.

The Jews Still Do Not Believe
-Jerusalem-
John 12:37-50

37 Although Jesus had performed so many miraculous signs before them, they still refused to believe in him, 38 so that the word of the prophet Isaiah would be fulfilled. He said, "Lord, who has believed our message, and to whom has the arm of the Lord been revealed?" 39 For this reason they could not believe, because again Isaiah said, 40 "He has blinded their eyes and hardened their heart, so that they would not see with their eyes and understand with their heart, and turn to me, and I would heal them." 41 Isaiah said these things because he saw Christ's glory, and spoke about him.

42 Nevertheless, even among the rulers many believed in him, but because of the Pharisees they would not confess Jesus to be the Christ, so that they would not be put out of the synagogue. 43 For they loved praise from men more than praise from God.

44 But Jesus shouted out, *"The one who believes in me does not believe in me, but in the one who sent me, 45 and the one who sees me sees the one who sent me. 46 I have come as a light into the world, so that everyone who believes in me should not remain in darkness." 47 "If anyone hears my words and does not obey them, I do not judge him. For I have not come to judge the world, but to save the world. 48 The one who rejects me and does not accept my words has a judge; the word I have spoken will judge him at the last day. 49 For I have not spoken from my own authority, but the Father himself who sent me has commanded me what I should say and what I should speak. 50 And I know that his commandment is eternal life. Thus, the things I say, I say just as the Father has told me."*

Withered Fig Tree and the Lesson on Faith
-Back to Bethany and return to Jerusalem-
Mark 11:19-25

19 When evening came, Jesus and his disciples went out of the city.

20 In the morning as they passed by, they saw the fig tree withered from the roots. 21 Peter remembered and said to him, "Rabbi, look! The fig tree you cursed has withered."

22 Jesus said to them, *"Have faith in God. 23 I tell you the truth, if someone says to this mountain, 'Be lifted up and thrown into the sea,' and does not doubt in his heart but believes that what he says will happen; it will be done for him. 24 For this reason I tell you, whatever you pray and ask for, believe that you have received it, and it will be yours. 25 Whenever you stand praying, if you have anything against anyone, forgive him, so that your Father in heaven will also forgive you your sins."*

The Challenge of Christ's Authority
-Jerusalem, in the Temple-
Luke 20:1-8

1 Now one day, as Jesus was teaching the people in the temple courts and proclaiming the gospel, the chief priests and the experts in the law with the elders came up 2 and said to him, "Tell us: By what authority are you doing these things? Or who it is who gave you this authority?" 3 He answered them, *"I will also ask you a question, and you tell me: 4 John's baptism – was it from heaven or from people?"* 5 So they discussed it with one another, saying, "If we say, 'From heaven,' he will say, 'Why did you not believe him?' 6 But if we say, 'From people,' all the people will stone us, because they are convinced that John was a prophet." 7 So they replied that they did not know where it came from. 8 Then Jesus said to them, *"Neither will I tell you by whose authority I do these things."*

The Parable of the Two Sons
-Jerusalem in the Temple-
Matthew 21:28-32

28 *"What do you think? A man had two sons. He went to the first and said, 'Son, go and work in the vineyard today.'"* 29 *"The boy answered, 'I will not.' But later he had a change of heart and went."* 30 *"The father went to the other son and said the same*

thing. This boy answered, 'I will, sir,' but did not go." 31 "Which of the two did his father's will?" They said, "The first." Jesus said to them, "I tell you the truth, tax collectors and prostitutes will go ahead of you into the kingdom of God! 32 For John came to you in the way of righteousness, and you did not believe him. But the tax collectors and prostitutes did believe. Although you saw this, you did not later change your minds and believe him."

The Parable of the Tenants
-Jerusalem in the Temple-
Matthew 21:33
33 "Listen to another parable: There was a landowner who planted a vineyard. He put a fence around it, dug a pit for its winepress, and built a watchtower. Then he leased it to tenant farmers and went on a journey."

Mark 12:2-6
2 "At harvest time he sent a slave to the tenants to collect from them his portion of the crop. 3 But those tenants seized his slave, beat him, and sent him away empty-handed. 4 So he sent another slave to them again. This one they struck on the head and treated outrageously. 5 He sent another, and that one they killed. This happened to many others, some of whom were beaten, others killed." 6 "He had one left, his one dear son. Finally, he sent him to them, saying, 'They will respect my son.'"

Matthew 21:38-46
38 "But when the tenants saw the son, they said to themselves, 'This is the heir. Come, let's kill him and get his inheritance!' 39 So they seized him, threw him out of the vineyard, and killed him." 40 "Now when the owner of the vineyard comes, what will he do to those tenants?" 41 They said to him, "He will utterly destroy those evil men! Then he will lease the vineyard to other tenants who will give him his portion at the harvest."

42 Jesus said to them, "Have you never read in the scriptures: 'The stone the builders rejected has become the cornerstone. This is from the Lord, and it is marvelous in our eyes'?"

43 "For this reason I tell you that the kingdom of God will be taken from you and given to a people who will produce its fruit. 44 The one who falls on this stone will be broken to pieces, and the one on whom it falls will be crushed." 45 When the chief priests and the Pharisees heard his parables, they realized that he was

speaking about them. 46 They wanted to arrest him, but they were afraid of the crowds, because the crowds regarded him as a prophet.

The Parable of the Wedding Banquet
-Jerusalem in the Temple-
Matthew 22:1-14

1 Jesus spoke to them again in parables, saying: *2 "The kingdom of heaven can be compared to a king who gave a wedding banquet for his son. 3 He sent his slaves to summon those who had been invited to the banquet, but they would not come." 4 "Again he sent other slaves, saying, 'Tell those who have been invited, "Look! The feast I have prepared for you is ready. My oxen and fattened cattle have been slaughtered, and everything is ready. Come to the wedding banquet."' 5 "But they were indifferent and went away, one to his farm, another to his business. 6 The rest seized his slaves, insolently mistreated them, and killed them. 7 The king was furious! He sent his soldiers, and they put those murderers to death and set their city on fire." 8 "Then he said to his slaves, 'The wedding is ready, but the ones who had been invited were not worthy. 9 So go into the main streets and invite everyone you find to the wedding banquet.' 10 And those slaves went out into the streets and gathered all they found, both bad and good, and the wedding hall was filled with guests." 11 "But when the king came in to see the wedding guests, he saw a man there who was not wearing wedding clothes. 12 And he said to him, 'Friend, how did you get in here without wedding clothes?' But he had nothing to say." 13 "Then the king said to his attendants, 'Tie him up hand and foot and throw him into the outer darkness, where there will be weeping and gnashing of teeth!'" 14 "For many are called, but few are chosen."*

Jesus Questioned About Paying Taxes to Caesar
-Jerusalem, probably in the Temple-
Matthew 22:15-22

15 Then the Pharisees went out and planned together to entrap him with his own words. 16 They sent to him their disciples along with the Herodians, saying, "Teacher, we know that you are truthful, and teach the way of God in accordance with the truth. You do not court anyone's favor because you show no partiality.

17 Tell us then, what do you think? Is it right to pay taxes to Caesar or not?"

18 But Jesus realized their evil intentions and said, *"Hypocrites! Why are you testing me? 19 Show me the coin used for the tax."* So they brought him a denarius. 20 Jesus said to them, *"Whose image is this, and whose inscription?"* 21 They replied, "Caesar's." He said to them, *"Then give to Caesar the things that are Caesar's, and to God the things that are God's."* 22 Now when they heard this they were stunned, and they left him and went away.

Marriage at the Resurrection
-Jerusalem, probably in the Temple-
Mark 12:18-24

18 Sadducees (who say there is no resurrection) also came to him and asked him, 19 "Teacher, Moses wrote for us: 'If a man's brother dies and leaves a wife but no children, that man must marry the widow and father children for his brother.' 20 There were seven brothers. The first one married, and when he died he had no children. 21 The second married her and died without any children, and likewise the third. 22 None of the seven had children. Finally, the woman died too. 23 In the resurrection, when they rise again, whose wife will she be? For all seven had married her." 24 Jesus said to them, *"Aren't you deceived for this reason, because you don't know the scriptures or the power of God?"*
Luke 20:34-40

34 So Jesus said to them, *"The people of this age marry and are given in marriage. 35 But those who are regarded as worthy to share in that age and in the resurrection from the dead neither marry nor are given in marriage. 36 In fact, they can no longer die, because they are equal to angels and are sons of God, since they are sons of the resurrection. 37 But even Moses revealed that the dead are raised in the passage about the bush, where he calls the Lord the God of Abraham and the God of Isaac and the God of Jacob. 38 Now he is not God of the dead, but of the living, for all live before him."* 39 Then some of the experts in the law answered, "Teacher, you have spoken well!" 40 For they did not dare any longer to ask him anything.

The Greatest Commandment
-Jerusalem, probably in the Temple-

34 Now when the Pharisees heard that he had silenced the Sadducees, they assembled together. 35 And one of them, an expert in religious law, asked him a question to test him: 36 "Teacher, which commandment in the law is the greatest?"

Mark 12:29-34

29 Jesus answered, *"The most important is: 'Listen, Israel, the Lord our God, the Lord is one. 30 Love the Lord your God with all your heart, with all your soul, with all your mind, and with all your strength.' 31 The second is: 'Love your neighbor as yourself.' There is no other commandment greater than these."* 32 The expert in the law said to him, "That is true, Teacher; you are right to say that he is one, and there is no one else besides him. 33 And to love him with all your heart, with all your mind, and with all your strength and to love your neighbor as yourself is more important than all burnt offerings and sacrifices." 34 When Jesus saw that he had answered thoughtfully, he said to him, *"You are not far from the kingdom of God."* Then no one dared any longer to question him.

Christ's Relationship to David
-Jerusalem, in the Temple-
Matthew 22:41-44

41 While the Pharisees were assembled, Jesus asked them a question: *42 "What do you think about the Christ? Whose son, is he?"* They said, "The son of David." 43 He said to them, *"How then does David by the Spirit call him 'Lord,' saying, 44 'The Lord said to my lord, "Sit at my right hand, until I put your enemies under your feet"'?*

Mark 12:37

37 "If David himself calls him 'Lord,' how can he be his son?" And the large crowd was listening to him with delight.

Seven Woes against the Scribes and Pharisees
-Jerusalem, in the Temple-
See Note: Empty
Matthew 23:1-36

1 Then Jesus said to the crowds and to his disciples, *2 "The experts in the law and the Pharisees sit on Moses' seat. 3 Therefore pay attention to what they tell you and do it. But do not do what they do, for they do not practice what they teach. 4 They*

tie up heavy loads, hard to carry, and put them on men's shoulders, but they themselves are not willing even to lift a finger to move them." 5 "They do all their deeds to be seen by people, for they make their phylacteries wide and their tassels long. 6 They love the place of honor at banquets and the best seats in the synagogues 7 and elaborate greetings in the marketplaces, and to have people call them 'Rabbi.'" 8 "But you are not to be called 'Rabbi,' for you have one Teacher and you are all brothers. 9 And call no one your 'father' on earth, for you have one Father, who is in heaven. 10 Nor are you to be called 'teacher,' for you have one teacher, the Christ. 11 The greatest among you will be your servant. 12 And whoever exalts himself will be humbled, and whoever humbles himself will be exalted."

13 "But woe to you, experts in the law and you Pharisees, hypocrites! You keep locking people out of the kingdom of heaven! For you neither enter nor permit those trying to enter to go in." 14 [[EMPTY]]

15 "Woe to you, experts in the law and you Pharisees, hypocrites! You cross land and sea to make one convert, and when you get one, you make him twice as much a child of hell as yourselves!"

16 "Woe to you, blind guides, who say, 'Whoever swears by the temple is bound by nothing. But whoever swears by the gold of the temple is bound by the oath.' 17 Blind fools! Which is greater, the gold or the temple that makes the gold sacred? 18 And, 'Whoever swears by the altar is bound by nothing. But if anyone swears by the gift on it he is bound by the oath.' 19 You are blind! For which is greater, the gift or the altar that makes the gift sacred? 20 So whoever swears by the altar swears by it and by everything on it. 21 And whoever swears by the temple swears by it and the one who dwells in it. 22 And whoever swears by heaven swears by the throne of God and the one who sits on it."

23 "Woe to you, experts in the law and you Pharisees, hypocrites! You give a tenth of mint, dill, and cumin, yet you neglect what is more important in the law – justice, mercy, and faithfulness! You should have done these things without neglecting the others. 24 Blind guides! You strain out a gnat yet swallow a camel!"

25 "Woe to you, experts in the law and you Pharisees, hypocrites! You clean the outside of the cup and the dish, but inside they are full of greed and self-indulgence. 26 Blind

Pharisee! First clean the inside of the cup, so that the outside may become clean too!"

27 "Woe to you, experts in the law and you Pharisees, hypocrites! You are like whitewashed tombs that look beautiful on the outside but inside are full of the bones of the dead and of everything unclean. 28 In the same way, on the outside you look righteous to people, but inside you are full of hypocrisy and lawlessness."

29 "Woe to you, experts in the law and you Pharisees, hypocrites! You build tombs for the prophets and decorate the graves of the righteous. 30 And you say, 'If we had lived in the days of our ancestors, we would not have participated with them in shedding the blood of the prophets.' 31 By saying this you testify against yourselves that you are descendants of those who murdered the prophets. 32 Fill up then the measure of your ancestors!" 33 "You snakes, you offspring of vipers! How will you escape being condemned to hell?

34 "For this reason I am sending you prophets and wise men and experts in the law, some of whom you will kill and crucify, and some you will flog in your synagogues and pursue from town to town, 35 so that on you will come all the righteous blood shed on earth, from the blood of righteous Abel to the blood of Zechariah son of Barachiah, whom you murdered between the temple and the altar. 36 I tell you the truth; this generation will be held responsible for all these things!"

Lament over Jerusalem
-Jerusalem, in the Temple-
Matthew 23:37-39

37 "O Jerusalem, Jerusalem, you who kill the prophets and stone those who are sent to you! How often I have longed to gather your children together as a hen gathers her chicks under her wings, but you would have none of it! 38 Look, your house is left to you desolate! 39 For I tell you, you will not see me from now until you say, 'Blessed is the one who comes in the name of the Lord!'"

A Poor Widow's Offering
-Jerusalem, in the Temple-
Mark 12:41-44

41 Then he sat down opposite the offering box, and watched the crowd putting coins into it. Many rich people were throwing in large amounts. 42 And a poor widow came and put in two small copper coins, worth less than a penny. 43 He called his disciples and said to them, *"I tell you the truth, this poor widow has put more into the offering box than all the others. 44 For they all gave out of their wealth. But she, out of her poverty, put in what she had to live on, everything she had."*

Signs of the End of the Age
-From the Temple to the Mount of Olives-
Mark 13:1-7

1 Now as Jesus was going out of the temple courts, one of his disciples said to him, "Teacher, look at these tremendous stones and buildings!" 2 Jesus said to him, *"Do you see these great buildings? Not one stone will be left on another. All will be torn down!"*

3 So while he was sitting on the Mount of Olives opposite the temple, Peter, James, John, and Andrew asked him privately, 4 "Tell us, when will these things happen? And what will be the sign that all these things are about to take place?" 5 Jesus began to say to them, *"Watch out that no one misleads you. 6 Many will come in my name, saying, 'I am he,' and they will mislead many. 7 When you hear of wars and rumors of wars, do not be alarmed. These things must happen, but the end is still to come."*

Luke 21:10-11

10 "Then he said to them, "Nation will rise up in arms against nation, and kingdom against kingdom. 11 There will be great earthquakes, and famines and plagues in various places, and there will be terrifying sights and great signs from heaven."

Mark 13:9-11

9 "You must watch out for yourselves. You will be handed over to councils and beaten in the synagogues. You will stand before governors and kings because of me, as a witness to them. 10 First the gospel must be preached to all nations. 11 When they arrest you and hand you over for trial, do not worry about what to speak. But say whatever is given you at that time, for it is not you speaking, but the Holy Spirit."

Matthew 24:10

10 "Then many will be led into sin, and they will betray one another and hate one another."

Mark 13:12

12 "Brother will hand over brother to death, and a father his child. Children will rise against parents and have them put to death."

Luke 21:17-19

17 "You will be hated by everyone because of my name. 18 Yet not a hair of your head will perish. 19 By your endurance you will gain your lives."

Matthew 24:11-14

11 "And many false prophets will appear and deceive many, 12 and because lawlessness will increase so much, the love of many will grow cold. 13 But the person who endures to the end will be saved. 14 And this gospel of the kingdom will be preached throughout the whole inhabited earth as a testimony to all the nations, and then the end will come."

Abomination of Desolation
-Mount of Olives-
Matthew 24:15-18

15 "So when you see the abomination of desolation – spoken about by Daniel the prophet – standing in the holy place (let the reader understand), 16 then those in Judea must flee to the mountains. 17 The one on the roof must not come down to take anything out of his house, 18 and the one in the field must not turn back to get his cloak."

Luke 21:22

22 "Because these are days of vengeance, to fulfill all that is written."

Mark 13:17-20

17 "Woe to those who are pregnant and to those who are nursing their babies in those days! 18 Pray that it may not be in winter. 19 For in those days there will be suffering unlike anything that has happened from the beginning of the creation that God created until now, or ever will happen. 20 And if the Lord had not cut short those days, no one would be saved. But because of the elect, whom he chose, he has cut them short."

Luke 21:23b-24

23b "For there will be great distress on the earth and wrath against this people. 24 They will fall by the edge of the sword and be led away as captives among all nations. Jerusalem will be trampled down by the Gentiles until the times of the Gentiles are fulfilled."

Matthew 24:23-28

23 "Then if anyone says to you, 'Look, here is the Christ!' or 'There he is!' do not believe him. 24 For false messiahs and false prophets will appear and perform great signs and wonders to deceive, if possible, even the elect. 25 Remember, I have told you ahead of time." 26 "So then, if someone says to you, 'Look, he is in the wilderness,' do not go out, or 'Look, he is in the inner rooms,' do not believe him. 27 For just like the lightning comes from the east and flashes to the west, so the coming of the Son of Man will be. 28 Wherever the corpse is, there the vultures will gather."

Coming of the Son of Man
-Mount of Olives-
Luke 21:25-26

25 "And there will be signs in the sun and moon and stars, and on the earth, nations will be in distress, anxious over the roaring of the sea and the surging waves. 26 People will be fainting from fear and from the expectation of what is coming on the world, for the powers of the heavens will be shaken."

Matthew 24:30-31

30 "Then the sign of the Son of Man will appear in heaven, and all the tribes of the earth will mourn. They will see the Son of Man arriving on the clouds of heaven with power and great glory. 31 And he will send his angels with a loud trumpet blast, and they will gather his elect from the four winds, from one end of heaven to the other."

Signs of Nearness
-Mount of Olives-
Luke 21:28-32

28 "But when these things begin to happen, stand up and raise your heads, because your redemption is drawing near."

29 Then he told them a parable: *"Look at the fig tree and all the other trees. 30 When they sprout leaves, you see for yourselves and know that summer is now near. 31 So also you, when you see these things happening, know that the kingdom of God is near." 32 "I tell you the truth; this generation will not pass away until all these things take place."*

Matthew 24:36-41

36 "But as for that day and hour no one knows it – not even the angels in heaven – except the Father alone. 37 For just like the days of Noah were, so the coming of the Son of Man will be. 38 For in those days before the flood, people were eating and drinking, marrying and giving in marriage, until the day Noah entered the ark. 39 And they knew nothing until the flood came and took them all away. It will be the same at the coming of the Son of Man. 40 Then there will be two men in the field; one will be taken and one left. 41 There will be two women grinding grain with a mill; one will be taken and one left."

Keep Watching and Keep Faithfull
-Mount of Olives-
Mark 13:32-37

32 "But as for that day or hour no one knows it – neither the angels in heaven, nor the Son – except the Father. 33 Watch out! Stay alert! For you do not know when the time will come. 34 It is like a man going on a journey. He left his house and put his slaves in charge, assigning to each his work, and commanded the doorkeeper to stay alert." 35 "Stay alert, then, because you do not know when the owner of the house will return – whether during evening, at midnight, when the rooster crows, or at dawn – 36 or else he might find you asleep when he returns suddenly. 37 What I say to you I say to everyone: Stay alert!"

Matthew 24:43-51

43 "But understand this: If the owner of the house had known at what time of night the thief was coming, he would have been alert and would not have let his house be broken into. 44 Therefore you also must be ready, because the Son of Man will come at an hour when you do not expect him."

45 "Who then is the faithful and wise slave, whom the master has put in charge of his household, to give the other slaves their food at the proper time? 46 Blessed is that slave whom the master finds at work when he comes. 47 I tell you the truth; the master will put him in charge of all his possessions. 48 But if that evil slave should say to himself, 'My master is staying away a long time,' 49 and he begins to beat his fellow slaves and to eat and drink with drunkards, 50 then the master of that slave will come on a day when he does not expect him and at an hour he does not foresee, 51 and will cut him in two, and assign him a place with the hypocrites, where there will be weeping and gnashing of teeth."

Luke 21:37-38

37 So every day Jesus was teaching in the temple courts, but at night he went and stayed on the Mount of Olives. 38 And all the people came to him early in the morning to listen to him in the temple courts.

The Parable of the Ten Virgins
-Mount of Olives-
Matthew 25:1-13

1 "At that time the kingdom of heaven will be like ten virgins who took their lamps and went out to meet the bridegroom. 2 Five of the virgins were foolish, and five were wise. 3 When the foolish ones took their lamps, they did not take extra olive oil with them. 4 But the wise ones took flasks of olive oil with their lamps. 5 When the bridegroom was delayed a long time, they all became drowsy and fell asleep." 6 "But at midnight there was a shout, 'Look, the bridegroom is here! Come out to meet him.'" 7 "Then all the virgins woke up and trimmed their lamps. 8 The foolish ones said to the wise, 'Give us some of your oil, because our lamps are going out.'" 9 "'No,' they replied. 'There won't be enough for you and for us. Go instead to those who sell oil and buy some for yourselves.'" 10 "But while they had gone to buy it, the bridegroom arrived, and those who were ready went inside with him to the wedding banquet. Then the door was shut." 11 "Later, the other virgins came too, saying, 'Lord, lord! Let us in!'" 12 "But he replied, 'I tell you the truth, I do not know you!'" 13 "Therefore stay alert, because you do not know the day or the hour."

Jesus Teaches Again About the Talents
-Mount of Olives-
Matthew 25:14-30

14 "For it is like a man going on a journey, who summoned his slaves and entrusted his property to them. 15 To one he gave five talents, to another two, and to another one, each according to his ability. Then he went on his journey. 16 The one who had received five talents went off right away and put his money to work and gained five more. 17 In the same way, the one who had two gained two more. 18 But the one who had received one talent went out

127 of 175

and dug a hole in the ground and hid his master's money in it." 19 "After a long time, the master of those slaves came and settled his accounts with them. 20 The one who had received the five talents came and brought five more, saying, 'Sir, you entrusted me with five talents. See, I have gained five more.'" 21 "His master answered, 'Well done, good and faithful slave! You have been faithful in a few things. I will put you in charge of many things. Enter into the joy of your master.'" 22 "The one with the two talents also came and said, 'Sir, you entrusted two talents to me. See, I have gained two more.'" 23 "His master answered, 'Well done, good and faithful slave! You have been faithful with a few things. I will put you in charge of many things. Enter into the joy of your master.'" 24 "Then the one who had received the one talent came and said, 'Sir, I knew that you were a hard man, harvesting where you did not sow, and gathering where you did not scatter seed, 25 so I was afraid, and I went and hid your talent in the ground. See, you have what is yours.'" 26 "But his master answered, 'Evil and lazy slave! So, you knew that I harvest where I didn't sow and gather where I didn't scatter? 27 Then you should have deposited my money with the bankers, and on my return, I would have received my money back with interest!" 28 "Therefore take the talent from him and give it to the one who has ten. 29 For the one who has will be given more, and he will have more than enough. But the one who does not have, even what he has will be taken from him. 30 And throw that worthless slave into the outer darkness, where there will be weeping and gnashing of teeth.'"

Separation of the Sheep from the Goats
-Mount of Olives-
Matthew 25:31-46

31 "When the Son of Man comes in his glory and all the angels with him, then he will sit on his glorious throne. 32 All the nations will be assembled before him, and he will separate people one from another like a shepherd separates the sheep from the goats. 33 He will put the sheep on his right and the goats on his left." 34 "Then the king will say to those on his right, 'Come, you who are blessed by my Father, inherit the kingdom prepared for you from the foundation of the world. 35 For I was hungry and you gave me food, I was thirsty and you gave me something to drink, I was a stranger and you invited me in, 36 I was naked and you gave me

clothing, I was sick and you took care of me, I was in prison and you visited me.'" 37 "Then the righteous will answer him, 'Lord, when did we see you hungry and feed you, or thirsty and give you something to drink? 38 When did we see you a stranger and invite you in, or naked and clothe you? 39 When did we see you sick or in prison and visit you?'" 40 "And the king will answer them, 'I tell you the truth, just as you did it for one of the least of these brothers or sisters of mine, you did it for me.'"

41 "Then he will say to those on his left, 'Depart from me, you accursed, into the eternal fire that has been prepared for the devil and his angels! 42 For I was hungry and you gave me nothing to eat, I was thirsty and you gave me nothing to drink. 43 I was a stranger and you did not receive me as a guest, naked and you did not clothe me, sick and in prison and you did not visit me.'" 44 "Then they too will answer, 'Lord, when did we see you hungry or thirsty or a stranger or naked or sick or in prison, and did not give you whatever you needed?'" 45 "Then he will answer them, 'I tell you the truth, just as you did not do it for one of the least of these, you did not do it for me.'" 46 "And these will depart into eternal punishment, but the righteous into eternal life."

Sanhedrin Plot to Arrest and Kill Jesus
-Mount of Olives and the court of the high priest-
Matthew 26:1-5
1 When Jesus had finished saying all these things, he told his disciples, *2 "You know that after two days the Passover is coming, and the Son of Man will be handed over to be crucified."* 3 Then the chief priests and the elders of the people met together in the palace of the high priest, who was named Caiaphas. 4 They planned to arrest Jesus by stealth and kill him. 5 But they said, "Not during the feast, so that there won't be a riot among the people."

Jesus Anointed Again at Bethany
-Bethany-
See Note: Jesus Anointed
Matthew 26:6-13
6 Now while Jesus was in Bethany at the house of Simon the leper, 7 a woman came to him with an alabaster jar of expensive perfumed oil, and she poured it on his head as he was at the table. 8 When the disciples saw this, they became indignant and said,

"Why this waste? 9 It could have been sold at a high price and the money given to the poor!" 10 When Jesus learned of this, he said to them, *"Why are you bothering this woman? She has done a good service for me. 11 For you will always have the poor with you, but you will not always have me! 12 When she poured this oil on my body, she did it to prepare me for burial. 13 I tell you the truth, wherever this gospel is proclaimed in the whole world, what she has done will also be told in memory of her."*

Judas' Agreement to Betray Jesus
-Jerusalem-
Luke 22:1-5

1 Now the Feast of Unleavened Bread, which is called the Passover, was approaching. 2 The chief priests and the experts in the law were trying to find some way to execute Jesus, for they were afraid of the people.

3 Then Satan entered Judas, the one called Iscariot, who was one of the twelve. 4 He went away and discussed with the chief priests and officers of the temple guard how he might betray Jesus, handing him over to them. 5 They were delighted and arranged to give him money.

Matthew 26:15

15 and said, "What will you give me to betray him into your hands?" So they set out thirty silver coins for him.

Luke 22:6

6 So Judas agreed and began looking for an opportunity to betray Jesus when no crowd was present.

Preparation for the Passover Meal
-Jerusalem-
Mark 14:12

12 Now on the first day of the feast of Unleavened Bread, when the Passover lamb is sacrificed, Jesus' disciples said to him, "Where do you want us to prepare for you to eat the Passover?"

Luke 22:8-13

8 Jesus sent Peter and John, saying, "Go and prepare the Passover for us to eat." 9 They said to him, "Where do you want us to prepare it?" 10 He said to them, *"Listen, when you have entered the city, a man carrying a jar of water will meet you. Follow him into the house that he enters 11 and tell the owner of the house, 'The Teacher says to you, "Where is the guest room*

where I may eat the Passover with my disciples?"' 12 Then he will show you a large furnished room upstairs. Make preparations there." 13 So they went and found things just as he had told them, and they prepared the Passover.

Beginning of the Passover Meal
-Jerusalem, in the Upper Room-
Luke 22:14-16

14 Now when the hour came, Jesus took his place at the table and the apostles joined him. 15 And he said to them, *"I have earnestly desired to eat this Passover with you before I suffer. 16 For I tell you, I will not eat it again until it is fulfilled in the kingdom of God."*

Jesus Washes the Disciples' Feet
-Jerusalem, in the Upper Room-
John13:1-20

1 Just before the Passover feast, Jesus knew that his time had come to depart from this world to the Father. Having loved his own who were in the world, he now loved them to the very end. 2 The evening meal was in progress, and the devil had already put into the heart of Judas Iscariot, Simon's son, that he should betray Jesus. 3 Because Jesus knew that the Father had handed all things over to him, and that he had come from God and was going back to God, 4 he got up from the meal, removed his outer clothes, took a towel and tied it around himself. 5 He poured water into the washbasin and began to wash the disciples' feet and to dry them with the towel he had wrapped around himself.

6 Then he came to Simon Peter. Peter said to him, "Lord, are you going to wash my feet?" 7 Jesus replied, *"You do not understand what I am doing now, but you will understand after these things."* 8 Peter said to him, "You will never wash my feet!" Jesus replied, *"If I do not wash you, you have no share with me."* 9 Simon Peter said to him, "Lord, wash not only my feet, but also my hands and my head!" 10 Jesus replied, *"The one who has bathed needs only to wash his feet, but is completely clean. And you disciples are clean, but not every one of you."* 11 (For Jesus knew the one who was going to betray him. For this reason he said, "Not every one of you is clean.")

12 So when Jesus had washed their feet and put his outer clothing back on, he took his place at the table again and said to

them, *"Do you understand what I have done for you? 13 You call me 'Teacher' and 'Lord,' and do so correctly, for that is what I am. 14 If I then, your Lord and Teacher, have washed your feet, you too ought to wash one another's feet. 15 For I have given you an example – you should do just as I have done for you. 16 I tell you the solemn truth, the slave is not greater than his master, nor is the one who is sent as a messenger greater than the one who sent him. 17 If you understand these things, you will be blessed if you do them."*

18 "What I am saying does not refer to all of you. I know the ones I have chosen. But this is to fulfill the scripture, 'The one who eats my bread has turned against me.' 19 I am telling you this now, before it happens, so that when it happens you may believe that I am he." 20 "I tell you the solemn truth, whoever accepts the one I send accepts me, and whoever accepts me accepts the one who sent me."

Identification of the Betrayer
-Jerusalem, in the Upper Room-
See Note: Judas Iscariot
John 13:21

21 When he had said these things, Jesus was greatly distressed in spirit, and testified, *"I tell you the solemn truth, one of you will betray me."*

Matthew 26:22-24

22 They became greatly distressed and each one began to say to him, "Surely not I, Lord?" 23 He answered, *"The one who has dipped his hand into the bowl with me will betray me. 24 The Son of Man will go as it is written about him, but woe to that man by whom the Son of Man is betrayed! It would be better for him if he had never been born."*

John 13:22-26

22 The disciples began to look at one another, worried and perplexed to know which of them he was talking about. 23 One of his disciples, the one Jesus loved, was at the table to the right of Jesus in a place of honor. 24 So Simon Peter gestured to this disciple to ask Jesus who it was he was referring to. 25 Then the disciple whom Jesus loved leaned back against Jesus' chest and asked him, "Lord, who is it?" 26 Jesus replied, *"It is the one to whom I will give this piece of bread after I have dipped it in the*

dish." Then he dipped the piece of bread in the dish and gave it to Judas Iscariot, Simon's son.

Matthew 26:25

25 Then Judas, the one who would betray him, said, "Surely not I, Rabbi?" Jesus replied, *"You have said it yourself."*

John 13:27-30

27 And after Judas took the piece of bread, Satan entered into him. Jesus said to him, *"What you are about to do, do quickly."* 28 (Now none of those present at the table understood why Jesus said this to Judas. 29 Some thought that, because Judas had the money box, Jesus was telling him to buy whatever they needed for the feast, or to give something to the poor.) 30 Judas took the piece of bread and went out immediately. (Now it was night.)

First Prediction of Peter's Denial
-Jerusalem, in the Upper Room-
John 13:31-38

31 When Judas had gone out, Jesus said, *"Now the Son of Man is glorified, and God is glorified in him. 32 If God is glorified in him, God will also glorify him in himself, and he will glorify him right away." 33 "Children, I am still with you for a little while. You will look for me, and just as I said to the Jewish religious leaders, 'Where I am going you cannot come,' now I tell you the same."*

34 "I give you a new commandment – to love one another. Just as I have loved you, you also are to love one another. 35 Everyone will know by this that you are my disciples – if you have love for one another."

36 Simon Peter said to him, "Lord, where are you going?" Jesus replied, *"Where I am going, you cannot follow me now, but you will follow later."* 37 Peter said to him, "Lord, why can't I follow you now? I will lay down my life for you!" 38 Jesus answered, *"Will you lay down your life for me? I tell you the solemn truth, the rooster will not crow until you have denied me three times!"*

Conclusion of the Meal
-Jerusalem, in the Upper Room-
Luke 22:17-20

17 Then he took a cup, and after giving thanks he said, *"Take this and divide it among yourselves. 18 For I tell you that from now on I will not drink of the fruit of the vine until the kingdom of*

God comes." 19 Then he took bread, and after giving thanks he broke it and gave it to them, saying, *"This is my body which is given for you. Do this in remembrance of me."* 20 And in the same way he took the cup after they had eaten, saying, *"This cup that is poured out for you is the new covenant in my blood."*

Dispute as to Which of them was Greatest
-Jerusalem, in the Upper Room-
Luke 22:24-32

24 A dispute also started among them over which of them was to be regarded as the greatest. 25 So Jesus said to them, *"The kings of the Gentiles lord it over them, and those in authority over them are called 'benefactors.' 26 Not so with you; instead the one who is greatest among you must become like the youngest, and the leader like the one who serves. 27 For who is greater, the one who is seated at the table, or the one who serves? Is it not the one who is seated at the table? But I am among you as one who serves."*

28 *"You are the ones who have remained with me in my trials. 29 Thus I grant to you a kingdom, just as my Father granted to me, 30 that you may eat and drink at my table in my kingdom, and you will sit on thrones judging the twelve tribes of Israel."*

31 *"Simon, Simon, pay attention! Satan has demanded to have you all, to sift you like wheat, 32 but I have prayed for you, Simon, that your faith may not fail. When you have turned back, strengthen your brothers."*

Jesus Tells His Disciples to Purchase a Sword
-Jerusalem, in the Upper Room-
Luke 22:35-38

35 Then Jesus said to them, *"When I sent you out with no money bag, or traveler's bag, or sandals, you didn't lack anything, did you?"* They replied, "Nothing." 36 He said to them, *"But now, the one who has a money bag must take it, and likewise a traveler's bag too. And the one who has no sword must sell his cloak and buy one. 37 For I tell you that this scripture must be fulfilled in me, 'And he was counted with the transgressors.' For what is written about me is being fulfilled."* 38 So they said, "Look, Lord, here are two swords." Then he told them, *"It is enough."*

Jesus Comforts His Disciples
-Jerusalem, in the Upper Room-

1 "Do not let your hearts be distressed. You believe in God; believe also in me. 2 There are many dwelling places in my Father's house. Otherwise, I would have told you, because I am going away to make ready a place for you. 3 And if I go and make ready a place for you, I will come again and take you to be with me, so that where I am you may be too. 4 And you know the way where I am going."

Jesus is the Way to the Father
-Jerusalem, in the Upper Room-
John 14:5-14

5 Thomas said, "Lord, we don't know where you are going. How can we know the way?" 6 Jesus replied, *"I am the way, and the truth, and the life. No one comes to the Father except through me. 7 If you have known me, you will know my Father too. And from now on you do know him and have seen him."*

8 Philip said, "Lord, show us the Father, and we will be content." 9 Jesus replied, *"Have I been with you for so long, and you have not known me, Philip? The person who has seen me has seen the Father! How can you say, 'Show us the Father'? 10 Do you not believe that I am in the Father, and the Father is in me? The words that I say to you, I do not speak on my own initiative, but the Father residing in me performs his miraculous deeds. 11 Believe me that I am in the Father, and the Father is in me, but if you do not believe me, believe because of the miraculous deeds themselves. 12 I tell you the solemn truth, the person who believes in me will perform the miraculous deeds that I am doing, and will perform greater deeds than these, because I am going to the Father. 13 And I will do whatever you ask in my name, so that the Father may be glorified in the Son. 14 If you ask me anything in my name, I will do it."*

Jesus Promises the Holy Spirit
-Jerusalem, in the Upper Room-
John 14:15-31

15 "If you love me, you will obey my commandments. 16 Then I will ask the Father, and he will give you another Advocate to be with you forever – 17 the Spirit of truth, whom the world cannot accept, because it does not see him or know him. But you know him, because he resides with you and will be in you.

18 I will not abandon you as orphans, I will come to you. 19 In a little while the world will not see me any longer, but you will see me; because I live, you will live too. 20 You will know at that time that I am in my Father and you are in me and I am in you. 21 The person who has my commandments and obeys them is the one who loves me. The one who loves me will be loved by my Father, and I will love him and will reveal myself to him." 22 "Lord," Judas (not Judas Iscariot) said, "what has happened that you are going to reveal yourself to us and not to the world?" 23 Jesus replied, *"If anyone loves me, he will obey my word, and my Father will love him, and we will come to him and take up residence with him. 24 The person who does not love me does not obey my words. And the word you hear is not mine, but the Father's who sent me."*

25 "I have spoken these things while staying with you. 26 But the Advocate, the Holy Spirit, whom the Father will send in my name, will teach you everything, and will cause you to remember everything I said to you."

27 "Peace I leave with you; my peace I give to you; I do not give it to you as the world does. Do not let your hearts be distressed or lacking in courage. 28 You heard me say to you, 'I am going away and I am coming back to you.' If you loved me, you would be glad that I am going to the Father, because the Father is greater than I am. 29 I have told you now before it happens, so that when it happens you may believe. 30 I will not speak with you much longer, for the ruler of this world is coming. He has no power over me, 31 but I am doing just what the Father commanded me, so that the world may know that I love the Father." "Get up, let us go from here."

Second Prediction of Peter's Denial
-Kidron Valley on the way to Gethsemane-
Matthew 26:30-35

30 After singing a hymn, they went out to the Mount of Olives.

31 Then Jesus said to them, *"This night you will all fall away because of me, for it is written:
'I will strike the shepherd, and the sheep of the flock will be scattered.' 32 But after I am raised, I will go ahead of you into Galilee."* 33 Peter said to him, "If they all fall away because of you, I will never fall away!" 34 Jesus said to him, *"I tell you the truth, on this night, before the rooster crows, you will deny me*

three times." 35 Peter said to him, "Even if I must die with you, I will never deny you." And all the disciples said the same thing.

The Vine and the Branches
-Kidron Valley on the way to Gethsemane-
John 15:1-17

1 "I am the true vine and my Father is the gardener. 2 He takes away every branch that does not bear fruit in me. He prunes every branch that bears fruit so that it will bear more fruit. 3 You are clean already because of the word that I have spoken to you. 4 Remain in me, and I will remain in you. Just as the branch cannot bear fruit by itself, unless it remains in the vine, so neither can you unless you remain in me."

5 "I am the vine; you are the branches. The one who remains in me – and I in him – bears much fruit, because apart from me you can accomplish nothing. 6 If anyone does not remain in me, he is thrown out like a branch, and dries up; and such branches are gathered up and thrown into the fire, and are burned up. 7 If you remain in me and my words remain in you, ask whatever you want, and it will be done for you. 8 My Father is honored by this, that you bear much fruit and show that you are my disciples."

9 "Just as the Father has loved me, I have also loved you; remain in my love. 10 If you obey my commandments, you will remain in my love, just as I have obeyed my Father's commandments and remain in his love. 11 I have told you these things so that my joy may be in you, and your joy may be complete. 12 My commandment is this – to love one another just as I have loved you. 13 No one has greater love than this – that one lays down his life for his friends. 14 You are my friends if you do what I command you. 15 I no longer call you slaves, because the slave does not understand what his master is doing. But I have called you friends, because I have revealed to you everything I heard from my Father. 16 You did not choose me, but I chose you and appointed you to go and bear fruit, fruit that remains, so that whatever you ask the Father in my name he will give you. 17 This I command you – to love one another."

The World Hates the Disciples
-Kidron Valley on the way to Gethsemane-
John 15:18-16:4

18 "If the world hates you, be aware that it hated me first. 19 If you belonged to the world, the world would love you as its own. However, because you do not belong to the world, but I chose you out of the world, for this reason the world hates you. 20 Remember what I told you, 'A slave is not greater than his master.' If they persecuted me, they will also persecute you. If they obeyed my word, they will obey yours too. 21 But they will do all these things to you on account of my name, because they do not know the one who sent me. 22 If I had not come and spoken to them, they would not be guilty of sin. But they no longer have any excuse for their sin. 23 The one who hates me hates my Father too. 24 If I had not performed among them the miraculous deeds that no one else did, they would not be guilty of sin. But now they have seen the deeds and have hated both me and my Father. 25 Now this happened to fulfill the word that is written in their law, 'They hated me without reason.'" 26 "When the Advocate comes, whom I will send you from the Father – the Spirit of truth who goes out from the Father – he will testify about me, 27 and you also will testify, because you have been with me from the beginning."

16:1 "I have told you all these things so that you will not fall away. 2 They will put you out of the synagogue, yet a time is coming when the one who kills you will think he is offering service to God. 3 They will do these things because they have not known the Father or me. 4 But I have told you these things so that when their time comes, you will remember that I told you about them."

"I did not tell you these things from the beginning because I was with you."

The Work of the Holy Spirit
-Kidron Valley on the way to Gethsemane-
John 16:5-15

5 "But now I am going to the one who sent me, and not one of you is asking me, 'Where are you going?' 6 Instead your hearts are filled with sadness because I have said these things to you. 7 But I tell you the truth; it is to your advantage that I am going away. For if I do not go away, the Advocate will not come to you, but if I go, I will send him to you. 8 And when he comes, he will prove the world wrong concerning sin and righteousness and judgment – 9 concerning sin, because they do not believe in me; 10 concerning righteousness, because I am going to the Father and you will see me no longer; 11 and concerning judgment, because the ruler of this world has been condemned."

12 "I have many more things to say to you, but you cannot bear them now. 13 But when he, the Spirit of truth, comes, he will guide you into all truth. For he will not speak on his own authority, but will speak whatever he hears, and will tell you what is to come. 14 He will glorify me, because he will receive from me what is mine and will tell it to you. 15 Everything that the Father has is mine; that is why I said the Spirit will receive from me what is mine and will tell it to you."

Prediction of Joy over His Resurrection
-Kidron Valley on the way to Gethsemane-
John 16:16-22

16 "In a little while you will see me no longer; again, after a little while, you will see me."

17 Then some of his disciples said to one another, "What is the meaning of what he is saying, *'In a little while you will not see me; again, after a little while, you will see me,'* and, *'because I am going to the Father'*?" 18 So they kept on repeating, "What is the meaning of what he says, *'In a little while'*? We do not understand what he is talking about."

19 Jesus could see that they wanted to ask him about these things, so he said to them, *"Are you asking each other about this – that I said, 'In a little while you will not see me; again, after a little while, you will see me'? 20 I tell you the solemn truth, you will weep and wail, but the world will rejoice; you will be sad, but your sadness will turn into joy. 21 When a woman gives birth, she has distress because her time has come, but when her child is born, she no longer remembers the suffering because of her joy that a human being has been born into the world. 22 So also you have sorrow now, but I will see you again, and your hearts will rejoice, and no one will take your joy away from you."*

Promise of Answered Prayer and Peace
-Kidron Valley on the way to Gethsemane-
John 16:23-33

23 "At that time you will ask me nothing. I tell you the solemn truth, whatever you ask the Father in my name he will give you. 24 Until now you have not asked for anything in my name. Ask and you will receive it, so that your joy may be complete."

25 "I have told you these things in obscure figures of speech; a time is coming when I will no longer speak to you in obscure figures, but will tell you plainly about the Father. 26 At that time you will ask in my name, and I do not say that I will ask the Father on your behalf. 27 For the Father himself loves you, because you have loved me and have believed that I came from God. 28 I came from the Father and entered into the world, but in turn, I am leaving the world and going back to the Father."

29 His disciples said, "Look, now you are speaking plainly and not in obscure figures of speech! 30 Now we know that you know everything and do not need anyone to ask you anything. Because of this we believe that you have come from God."

31 Jesus replied, *"Do you now believe? 32 Look, a time is coming – and has come – when you will be scattered, each one to his own home, and I will be left alone. Yet I am not alone, because my Father is with me." 33 "I have told you these things so that in me you may have peace. In the world you have trouble and suffering, but take courage – I have conquered the world."*

Jesus Prays for Himself
-Kidron Valley on the way to Gethsemane-
John 17:1-5

1 When Jesus had finished saying these things; he looked upward to heaven and said, *"Father, the time has come. Glorify your Son, so that your Son may glorify you – 2 just as you have given him authority over all humanity, so that he may give eternal life to everyone you have given him. 3 Now this is eternal life – that they know you, the only true God, and Jesus Christ, whom you sent. 4 I glorified you on earth by completing the work you gave me to do. 5 And now, Father, glorify me at your side with the glory I had with you before the world was created."*

Jesus Prays for His Disciples
-Kidron Valley on the way to Gethsemane-
John 17:6-19

6 "I have revealed your name to the men you gave me out of the world. They belonged to you, and you gave them to me, and they have obeyed your word. 7 Now they understand that everything you have given me comes from you, 8 because I have given them the words you have given me. They accepted them and really understand that I came from you, and they believed that you sent me. 9 I am praying on behalf of them. I am not praying on behalf of the world, but on behalf of those you have given me, because they belong to you. 10 Everything I have belongs to you, and everything you have belongs to me, and I have been glorified by them. 11 I am no longer in the world, but they are in the world, and I am coming to you. Holy Father, keep them safe in your name that you have given me, so that they may be one just as we are one. 12 When I was with them I kept them safe and watched over them in your name that you have given me. Not one of them was lost except the one destined for destruction, so that the scripture could be fulfilled." 13 "But now I am coming to you, and I am saying these things in the world, so they may experience my joy completed in themselves. 14 I have given them your word, and the world has hated them, because they do not belong to the world, just as I do not belong to the world. 15 I am not asking you to take them out of the world, but that you keep them safe from the evil one. 16 They do not belong to the world just as I do not belong to the world. 17 Set them apart in the truth; your word is truth. 18 Just as you sent me into the world, so I sent them into the world. 19 And I set myself apart on their behalf, so that they too may be truly set apart."

Jesus Prays for All Believers
-Kidron Valley on the way to Gethsemane-
John 17:20-18:1

20 "I am not praying only on their behalf, but also on behalf of those who believe in me through their testimony, 21 that they will all be one, just as you, Father, are in me and I am in you. I pray that they will be in us, so that the world will believe that you sent me. 22 The glory you gave to me I have given to them, that they may be one just as we are one – 23 I in them and you in me – that they may be completely one, so that the world will know that you sent me, and you have loved them just as you have loved me."

24 "Father, I want those you have given me to be with me where I am, so that they can see my glory that you gave me because you loved me before the creation of the world." 25 "Righteous Father, even if the world does not know you, I know you, and these men know that you sent me. 26 I made known your name to them, and I will continue to make it known, so that the love you have loved me with may be in them, and I may be in them."

18:1 When he had said these things, Jesus went out with his disciples across the Kidron Valley. There was an orchard there, and he and his disciples went into it.

Jesus Prays in the Garden of Gethsemane
-Garden of Gethsemane on the Mount of Olives -
Mark 14:32-36
32 Then they went to a place called Gethsemane, and Jesus said to his disciples, *"Sit here while I pray."* 33 He took Peter, James, and John with him, and became very troubled and distressed. 34 He said to them, *"My soul is deeply grieved, even to the point of death. Remain here and stay alert."* 35 Going a little farther, he threw himself to the ground and prayed that if it were possible the hour would pass from him. 36 He said, *"Abba, Father, all things are possible for you. Take this cup away from me. Yet not what I will, but what you will."*

Luke 22:43-44
43 [Then an angel from heaven appeared to him and strengthened him. 44 And in his anguish he prayed more earnestly, and his sweat was like drops of blood falling to the ground.]

Matthew 26:40-46
40 Then he came to the disciples and found them sleeping. He said to Peter, *"So, couldn't you stay awake with me for one hour? 41 Stay awake and pray that you will not fall into temptation. The spirit is willing, but the flesh is weak."* 42 He went away a second time and prayed, *"My Father, if this cup cannot be taken away unless I drink it, your will must be done."* 43 He came again and found them sleeping; they could not keep their eyes open. 44 So leaving them again, he went away and prayed for the third time, saying the same thing once more. 45 Then he came to the disciples and said to them, *"Are you still sleeping and resting? Look, the hour is approaching, and the Son of Man is betrayed into the hands of sinners. 46 Get up, let us go. Look! My betrayer is approaching!"*

Jesus Betrayed, Arrested, and Forsaken
-Gethsemane-
John 18:2-9
2 (Now Judas, the one who betrayed him, knew the place too, because Jesus had met there many times with his disciples.) 3 So Judas obtained a squad of soldiers and some officers of the chief

priests and Pharisees. They came to the orchard with lanterns and torches and weapons.

4 Then Jesus, because he knew everything that was going to happen to him, came and asked them, *"Who are you looking for?"* 5 They replied, "Jesus the Nazarene." He told them, "I am he." (Now Judas, the one who betrayed him, was standing there with them.) 6 So when Jesus said to them, *"I am he,"* they retreated and fell to the ground. 7 Then Jesus asked them again, *"Who are you looking for?"* And they said, "Jesus the Nazarene." 8 Jesus replied, *"I told you that I am he. If you are looking for me, let these men go."* 9 He said this to fulfill the word he had spoken, *"I have not lost a single one of those whom you gave me."*

Mark 14:44-45

44 (Now the betrayer had given them a sign, saying, "The one I kiss is the man. Arrest him and lead him away under guard.") 45 When Judas arrived, he went up to Jesus immediately and said, "Rabbi!" and kissed him.

Luke 22:48

48 But Jesus said to him, *"Judas, would you betray the Son of Man with a kiss?"*

Matthew 26:50

50 Jesus said to him, *"Friend, do what you are here to do."* Then they came and took hold of Jesus and arrested him.

Luke 22:49

49 When those who were around him saw what was about to happen, they said, "Lord, should we use our swords?"

John 18:10-11

10 Then Simon Peter, who had a sword, pulled it out and struck the high priest's slave, cutting off his right ear. (Now the slave's name was Malchus.) 11 But Jesus said to Peter, *"Put your sword back into its sheath! Am I not to drink the cup that the Father has given me?"*

Luke 22:51

51 But Jesus said, *"Enough of this!"* And he touched the man's ear and healed him.

Matthew 26:53-56

53 Or do you think that I cannot call on my Father, and that he would send me more than twelve legions of angels right now? 54 How then would the scriptures that say it must happen this way be fulfilled?" 55 At that moment Jesus said to the crowd, *"Have you come out with swords and clubs to arrest me like you would an outlaw? Day after day I sat teaching in the temple courts, yet you did not arrest me. 56 But this has happened so that the scriptures of the prophets would be fulfilled."* Then all the disciples left him and fled.

John 18:12

12 Then the squad of soldiers with their commanding officer and the officers of the Jewish leaders arrested Jesus and tied him up.

Mark 14:51-52

51 A young man was following him, wearing only a linen cloth. They tried to arrest him, 52 but he ran off naked, leaving his linen cloth behind.

Jesus Taken Before Annas
-Jerusalem, Court of Annas-
John 18:13-14

13 They brought him first to Annas, for he was the father-in-law of Caiaphas, who was high priest that year. 14 (Now it was Caiaphas who had advised the Jewish leaders that it was to their advantage that one man die for the people.)

Peter's First Denial
-Jerusalem, Court of Annas-
See Note: Peter's Denials
John 18:15-18

15 Simon Peter and another disciple followed them as they brought Jesus to Annas. (Now the other disciple was acquainted with the high priest, and he went with Jesus into the high priest's courtyard.) 16 But Simon Peter was left standing outside by the door. So the other disciple who was acquainted with the high priest came out and spoke to the slave girl who watched the door, and brought Peter inside. 17 The girl who was the doorkeeper said to Peter, "You're not one of this man's disciples too, are you?" He replied, "I am not." 18 (Now the slaves and the guards were standing around a charcoal fire they had made, warming themselves because it was cold. Peter also was standing with them, warming himself.)

Jesus Questioned by the High Priest
-Jerusalem, Court of Annas-
John 18:19-24

19 While this was happening, the high priest questioned Jesus about his disciples and about his teaching. 20 Jesus replied, *"I have spoken publicly to the world. I always taught in the synagogues and in the temple courts, where all the Jewish people assemble together. I have said nothing in secret. 21 Why do you ask me? Ask those who heard what I said. They know what I said."* 22 When Jesus had said this, one of the high priest's officers who stood nearby struck him on the face and said, "Is that the way you answer the high priest?" 23 Jesus replied, *"If I have said something wrong, confirm what is wrong. But if I spoke correctly, why strike me?"* 24 Then Annas sent him, still tied up, to Caiaphas the high priest.

Jesus Taken Before Caiaphas and the Sanhedrin
-Jerusalem, House of Caiaphas-
Matthew 26:57

57 Now the ones who had arrested Jesus led him to Caiaphas, the high priest, in whose house the experts in the law and the elders had gathered.

Mark 14:54-65

54 And Peter had followed him from a distance, up to the high priest's courtyard. He was sitting with the guards and warming himself by the fire. 55 The chief priests and the whole Sanhedrin were looking for evidence against Jesus so that they could put him to death, but they did not find anything. 56 Many gave false testimony against him, but their testimony did not agree. 57 Some stood up and gave this false testimony against him: 58 "We heard him say, 'I will destroy this temple made with hands and in three days build another not made with hands.'" 59 Yet even on this point their testimony did not agree. 60 Then the high priest stood up before them and asked Jesus, "Have you no answer? What is this that they are testifying against you?" 61 But he was silent and did not answer. Again, the high priest questioned him, "Are you the Christ, the Son of the Blessed One?" 62 *"I am,"* said Jesus, *"and you will see the Son of Man sitting at the right hand of the Power and coming with the clouds of heaven."* 63 Then the high priest tore his clothes and said, "Why do we still need witnesses? 64 You have heard the blasphemy! What is your verdict?" They all condemned him as deserving death. 65 Then some began to spit on him, and to blindfold him, and to strike him with their fists, saying, "Prophesy!" The guards also took him and beat him.

Peter's Second Denial
-Jerusalem, Courtyard of Caiaphas-
See Note: Peter's Denials
John 18:25

25 Meanwhile Simon Peter was standing in the courtyard warming himself. They said to him, "You aren't one of his disciples too, are you?" Peter denied it: "I am not!"

Matthew 26:71-72

71 When he went out to the gateway, another slave girl saw him and said to the people there, "This man was with Jesus the Nazarene." 72 He denied it again with an oath, "I do not know the man!"

Luke 22:58

58 Then a little later someone else saw him and said, "You are one of them too."
But Peter said, "Man, I am not!"

Peter's Third Denial
-Jerusalem, Courtyard of Caiaphas-
See Note: Peter's Denials
Luke 22:59

59 And after about an hour still another insisted, "Certainly this man was with him, because he too is a Galilean."

John 18:26

26 One of the high priest's slaves, a relative of the man whose ear Peter had cut off, said, "Did I not see you in the orchard with him?"

Luke 22:60a

60a But Peter said, "Man, I don't know what you're talking about!"

Matthew 26:74a

74a At that he began to curse, and he swore with an oath, "I do not know the man!"

Luke 22: 60b-62

60b At that moment, while he was still speaking, a rooster crowed. 61 Then the Lord turned and looked straight at Peter, and Peter remembered the word of the Lord, how he had said to him, *"Before a rooster crows today, you will deny me three times."* 62 And he went outside and wept bitterly.

The Guards Mock Jesus
-Jerusalem, courtyard of Caiaphas-
Luke 22:63-65

63 Now the men who were holding Jesus under guard began to mock him and beat him. 64 They blindfolded him and asked him repeatedly, "Prophesy! Who hit you?" 65 They also said many other things against him, reviling him.

Jesus Taken Before the Sanhedrin
-Jerusalem, meeting place of Sanhedrin-
Luke 22:66-71

66 When day came, the council of the elders of the people gathered together, both the chief priests and the experts in the law. Then they led Jesus away to their council 67 and said, "If you are the Christ, tell us." But he said to them, *"If I tell you, you will not believe, 68 and if I ask you, you will not answer. 69 But from now on the Son of Man will be seated at the right hand of the power of God."*

70 So they all said, "Are you the Son of God, then?" He answered them, *"You say that I am."* 71 Then they said, "Why do we need further testimony? We have heard it ourselves from his own lips!"

Remorse and Suicide of Judas Iscariot
-In the Temple and the Potter's Field-
Matthew 27:3-10

3 Now when Judas, who had betrayed him, saw that Jesus had been condemned, he regretted what he had done and returned the thirty silver coins to the chief priests and the elders, 4 saying, "I have sinned by betraying innocent blood!" But they said, "What is that to us? You take care of it yourself!" 5 So Judas threw the silver coins into the temple and left. Then he went out and hanged himself. 6 The chief priests took the silver and said, "It is not lawful to put this into the temple treasury, since it is blood money." 7 After consulting together they bought the Potter's Field with it, as a burial place for foreigners. 8 For this reason that field has been called the "Field of Blood" to this day. 9 Then what was spoken by Jeremiah the prophet was fulfilled: "They took the thirty silver coins, the price of the one whose price had been set by the people of Israel, 10 and they gave them for the potter's field, as the Lord commanded me."

Jesus Taken Before Pilate the First Time
-Jerusalem, at the Praetorium-
John 18:28-30

28 Then they brought Jesus from Caiaphas to the Roman governor's residence. (Now it was very early morning.) They did not go into the governor's residence so they would not be ceremonially defiled, but could eat the Passover meal. 29 So Pilate came outside to them and said, "What accusation do you bring against this man?" 30 They replied, "If this man were not a criminal, we would not have handed him over to you."

Luke 23:2-3

2 They began to accuse him, saying, "We found this man subverting our nation, forbidding us to pay the tribute tax to Caesar and claiming that he himself is Christ, a king. 3 So Pilate asked Jesus, "Are you the king of the Jews?" He replied, *"You say so."*

Matthew 27:12-14

12 But when he was accused by the chief priests and the elders, he did not respond. 13 Then Pilate said to him, "Don't you hear how many charges they are bringing against you?" 14 But he did not answer even one accusation, so that the governor was quite amazed.

John 18:31-38

31 Pilate told them "Take him yourselves and pass judgment on him according to your own law!"

The Jewish leaders replied, "We cannot legally put anyone to death." 32 (This happened to fulfill the word Jesus had spoken when he indicated what kind of death he was going to die.)

33 So Pilate went back into the governor's residence, summoned Jesus, and asked him, "Are you the king of the Jews?" 34 Jesus replied, *"Are you saying this on your own initiative, or have others told you about me?"* 35 Pilate answered, "I am not a Jew, am I? Your own people and your chief priests handed you over to me. What have you done?"

36 Jesus replied, *"My kingdom is not from this world. If my kingdom were from this world, my servants would be fighting to keep me from being handed over to the Jewish authorities. But as it is, my kingdom is not from here."* 37 Then Pilate said, "So you are a king!" Jesus replied, *"You say that I am a king. For this reason, I was born, and for this reason I came into the world – to*

testify to the truth. Everyone who belongs to the truth listens to my voice." 38 Pilate asked, "What is truth?"

When he had said this he went back outside to the Jewish leaders and announced, "I find no basis for an accusation against him.

Luke 23:5-7

5 But they persisted in saying, "He incites the people by teaching throughout all Judea. It started in Galilee and ended up here!"

6 Now when Pilate heard this, he asked whether the man was a Galilean. 7 When he learned that he was from Herod's jurisdiction, he sent him over to Herod, who also happened to be in Jerusalem at that time.

Jesus Taken Before Herod Antipas
-Jerusalem, before Herod Antipas-
Luke 23:8-12

8 When Herod saw Jesus, he was very glad, for he had long desired to see him, because he had heard about him and was hoping to see him perform some miraculous sign. 9 So Herod questioned him at considerable length; Jesus gave him no answer. 10 The chief priests and the experts in the law were there, vehemently accusing him. 11 Even Herod with his soldiers treated him with contempt and mocked him. Then, dressing him in elegant clothes, Herod sent him back to Pilate. 12 That very day Herod and Pilate became friends with each other, for prior to this they had been enemies.

Jesus Taken Before Pilate the Second Time
-Jerusalem, at the Praetorium-
Luke 23:13-16

13 Then Pilate called together the chief priests, the rulers, and the people, 14 and said to them, "You brought me this man as one who was misleading the people. When I examined him before you, I did not find this man guilty of anything you accused him of doing. 15 Neither did Herod, for he sent him back to us. Look, he has done nothing deserving death 16 I will therefore have him flogged and release him."

Matthew 27:15-16

15 During the feast the governor was accustomed to release one prisoner to the crowd, whomever they wanted. 16 At that time they had in custody a notorious prisoner named Jesus Barabbas.

19 (This was a man who had been thrown into prison for an insurrection started in the city, and for murder.)

Mark 15:8-10
8 Then the crowd came up and began to ask Pilate to release a prisoner for them, as was his custom. 9 So Pilate asked them, "Do you want me to release the king of the Jews for you?" 10 (For he knew that the chief priests had handed him over because of envy.)

Matthew 27:19-21
19 As he was sitting on the judgment seat, his wife sent a message to him: "Have nothing to do with that innocent man; I have suffered greatly as a result of a dream about him today." 20 But the chief priests and the elders persuaded the crowds to ask for Barabbas and to have Jesus killed. 21 The governor asked them, "Which of the two do you want me to release for you?" And they said, "Barabbas!"

Mark 15:12-14
12 So Pilate spoke to them again, "Then what do you want me to do with the one you call king of the Jews?" 13 They shouted back, "Crucify him!" 14 Pilate asked them, "Why? What has he done wrong?" But they shouted more insistently, "Crucify him!

Luke 23:20-23
20 Pilate addressed them once again because he wanted to release Jesus. 21 But they kept on shouting, "Crucify, crucify him!" 22 A third time he said to them, "Why? What wrong has he done? I have found him guilty of no crime deserving death. I will therefore flog him and release him." 23 But they were insistent, demanding with loud shouts that he be crucified. And their shouts prevailed.

Matthew 27:24-30
24 When Pilate saw that he could do nothing, but that instead a riot was starting, he took some water, washed his hands before the crowd and said, "I am innocent of this man's blood. You take care of it yourselves!" 25 In reply all the people said, "Let his blood be on us and on our children!" 26 Then he released Barabbas for them. But after he had Jesus flogged, he handed him over to be crucified. 27 Then the governor's soldiers took Jesus into the governor's residence and gathered the whole cohort around him. 28 They stripped him and put a scarlet robe around him, 29 and after braiding a crown of thorns, they put it on his head. They put a staff in his right hand, and kneeling down before him, they

mocked him: "Hail, king of the Jews!" 30 They spat on him and took the staff and struck him repeatedly on the head.

John 19:4-16a

4 Again Pilate went out and said to the Jewish leaders, "Look, I am bringing him out to you, so that you may know that I find no reason for an accusation against him." 5 So Jesus came outside, wearing the crown of thorns and the purple robe. Pilate said to them, "Look, here is the man!" 6 When the chief priests and their officers saw him, they shouted out, "Crucify him! Crucify him!" Pilate said, "You take him and crucify him! Certainly I find no reason for an accusation against him!" 7 The Jewish leaders replied, "We have a law, and according to our law he ought to die, because he claimed to be the Son of God!"

8 When Pilate heard what they said, he was more afraid than ever, 9 and he went back into the governor's residence and said to Jesus, "Where do you come from?" But Jesus gave him no answer. 10 So Pilate said, "Do you refuse to speak to me? Don't you know I have the authority to release you, and to crucify you?" 1 Jesus replied, *"You would have no authority over me at all, unless it was given to you from above. Therefore, the one who handed me over to you is guilty of greater sin."*

12 From this point on, Pilate tried to release him. But the Jewish leaders shouted out, "If you release this man, you are no friend of Caesar! Everyone who claims to be a king opposes Caesar!" 13 When Pilate heard these words he brought Jesus outside and sat down on the judgment seat in the place called "The Stone Pavement" (Gabbatha in Aramaic). 14 (Now it was the day of preparation for the Passover, about noon.) Pilate said to the Jewish leaders, "Look, here is your king!"

15 Then they shouted out, "Away with him! Away with him! Crucify him!" Pilate asked, "Shall I crucify your king?" The high priests replied, "We have no king except Caesar!" 16a Then Pilate handed him over to them to be crucified.

Mark 15:20

20 When they had finished mocking him, they stripped him of the purple cloak and put his own clothes back on him. Then they led him away to crucify him.

Journey to Golgotha
-Jerusalem-
Mark 15:21

21 The soldiers forced a passerby to carry his cross, Simon of Cyrene, who was coming in from the country (he was the father of Alexander and Rufus).

Luke 23:27-32

27 A great number of the people followed him, among them women who were mourning and wailing for him. 28 But Jesus turned to them and said, *"Daughters of Jerusalem, do not weep for me, but weep for yourselves and for your children. 29 For this is certain: The days are coming when they will say, 'Blessed are the barren, the wombs that never bore children, and the breasts that never nursed!' 30 Then they will begin to say to the mountains, 'Fall on us!' and to the hills, 'Cover us!' 31 For if such things are done when the wood is green, what will happen when it is dry?"*

32 Two other criminals were also led away to be executed with him.

Matthew 27:33-34

33 They came to a place called Golgotha (which means "Place of the Skull") 34 and offered Jesus wine mixed with gall to drink. But after tasting it, he would not drink it.

First Three Hours of Crucifixion
-Jerusalem, Golgotha-

John 19:18

18 There they crucified him along with two others, one on each side, with Jesus in the middle.

Luke 23:34

34 [But Jesus said, *"Father, forgive them, for they don't know what they are doing."*] Then they threw dice to divide his clothes.

John 19:19-24

19 Pilate also had a notice written and fastened to the cross, which read: "Jesus the Nazarene, the king of the Jews." 20 Thus many of the Jewish residents of Jerusalem read this notice, because the place where Jesus was crucified was near the city, and the notice was written in Aramaic, Latin, and Greek. 21 Then the chief priests of the Jews said to Pilate, "Do not write, 'The king of the Jews,' but rather, 'This man said, I am king of the Jews.'" 22 Pilate answered, "What I have written, I have written."

23 Now when the soldiers crucified Jesus, they took his clothes and made four shares, one for each soldier, and the tunic remained. (Now the tunic was seamless, woven from top to bottom as a single piece.) 24 So the soldiers said to one another,

"Let's not tear it, but throw dice to see who will get it." This took place to fulfill the scripture that says, "They divided my garments among them, and for my clothing they threw dice." So the soldiers did these things.

Matthew 27:36-37

36 Then they sat down and kept guard over him there. 37 Above his head they put the charge against him, which read: "This is Jesus, the king of the Jews."

Matthew 27:39-44

39 Those who passed by defamed him, shaking their heads 40 and saying, "You who can destroy the temple and rebuild it in three days, save yourself! If you are God's Son, come down from the cross!" 41 In the same way even the chief priests – together with the experts in the law and elders – were mocking him: 42 "He saved others, but he cannot save himself! He is the king of Israel! If he comes down now from the cross, we will believe in him! 43 He trusts in God – let God, if he wants to, deliver him now because he said, 'I am God's Son'!" 44 The robbers who were crucified with him also spoke abusively to him.

Luke 23:35-43

35 The people also stood there watching, but the rulers ridiculed him, saying, "He saved others. Let him save himself if he is the Christ of God, his chosen one!" 36 The soldiers also mocked him, coming up and offering him sour wine, 37 and saying, "If you are the king of the Jews, save yourself!" 38 There was also an inscription over him, "This is the king of the Jews."

39 One of the criminals who was hanging there railed at him, saying, "Aren't you the Christ? Save yourself and us!" 40 But the other rebuked him, saying, "Don't you fear God, since you are under the same sentence of condemnation? 41 And we rightly so, for we are getting what we deserve for what we did, but this man has done nothing wrong." 42 Then he said, "Jesus, remember me when you come in your kingdom." 43 And Jesus said to him, *"I tell you the truth, today you will be with me in paradise."*

John 19:25-27

25 Now standing beside Jesus' cross were his mother, his mother's sister, Mary the wife of Clopas, and Mary Magdalene. 26 So when Jesus saw his mother and the disciple whom he loved standing there, he said to his mother, *"Woman, look, here is your son!"* 27 He then said to his disciple, *"Look, here is your*

mother!" From that very time the disciple took her into his own home.

Last Three Hours of Crucifixion
-Jerusalem, Golgotha-
Matthew 27:45-49

45 Now from noon until three, darkness came over all the land. 46 At about three o'clock Jesus shouted with a loud voice,?" *"Eli, Eli, lema sabachthani?"* that is, *"My God, my God, why have you forsaken me?"* 47 When some of the bystanders heard it, they said, "This man is calling for Elijah." 48 Immediately one of them ran and got a sponge, filled it with sour wine, put it on a stick, and gave it to him to drink. 49 But the rest said, "Leave him alone! Let's see if Elijah will come to save him."

John 19:28-30a

28 After this Jesus, realizing that by this time everything was completed, said (in order to fulfill the scripture), *"I am thirsty!"* 29 A jar full of sour wine was there, so they put a sponge soaked in sour wine on a branch of hyssop and lifted it to his mouth. 30a When he had received the sour wine, Jesus said, *"It is completed!"*

Luke 23:46

46 Then Jesus, calling out with a loud voice, said, *"Father, into your hands I commit my spirit!"* And after he said this he breathed his last.

Matthew 27:51-54

51 Just then the temple curtain was torn in two, from top to bottom. The earth shook and the rocks were split apart. 52 And tombs were opened, and the bodies of many saints who had died were raised. 53 (They came out of the tombs after his resurrection and went into the holy city and appeared too many people.) 54 Now when the centurion and those with him who were guarding Jesus saw the earthquake and what took place, they were extremely terrified and said, "Truly this one was God's Son!"

Mark 15:40-41

40 There were also women, watching from a distance. Among them were Mary Magdalene, and Mary the mother of James the younger and of Joses, and Salome. 41 When he was in Galilee, they had followed him and given him support. Many other women who had come up with him to Jerusalem were there too.

Certification of the Death of Jesus
-Golgotha and the Praetorium-
John 19:31-37

31 Then, because it was the day of preparation, so that the bodies should not stay on the crosses on the Sabbath (for that Sabbath was an especially important one), the Jewish leaders asked Pilate to have the victims' legs broken and the bodies taken down. 32 So the soldiers came and broke the legs of the two men who had been crucified with Jesus, first the one and then the other. 33 But when they came to Jesus and saw that he was already dead, they did not break his legs. 34 But one of the soldiers pierced his side with a spear, and blood and water flowed out immediately. 35 And the person who saw it has testified (and his testimony is true, and he knows that he is telling the truth), so that you also may believe. 36 For these things happened so that the scripture would be fulfilled, "Not a bone of his will be broken." 37 And again another scripture says, "They will look on the one whom they have pierced."

Jesus' Body Placed in a Tomb
-The Garden Tomb at Golgotha-
Mark 15:42

42 Now when evening had already come, since it was the day of preparation (that is, the day before the Sabbath).
Luke 23:50-52
50 Now there was a man named Joseph who was a member of the council, a good and righteous man. 51 (He had not consented to their plan and action.) He was from the Judean town of Arimathea, and was looking forward to the kingdom of God. 52 He went to Pilate and asked for the body of Jesus.
Mark 15:44-46a
44 Pilate was surprised that he was already dead. He called the centurion and asked him if he had been dead for some time. 45 When Pilate was informed by the centurion, he gave the body to Joseph. 46a After Joseph bought a linen cloth and took down the body, he wrapped it in the linen.
John 19:39-42
39 Nicodemus, the man who had previously come to Jesus at night, accompanied Joseph, carrying a mixture of myrrh and aloes weighing about seventy-five pounds. 40 Then they took Jesus' body and wrapped it, with the aromatic spices, in strips of linen

cloth according to Jewish burial customs. 41 Now at the place where Jesus was crucified there was a garden, and in the garden was a new tomb where no one had yet been buried. 42 And so, because it was the Jewish day of preparation and the tomb was nearby, they placed Jesus' body there.

Matthew 27:59-60
59 Joseph took the body, wrapped it in a clean linen cloth, 60 and placed it in his own new tomb that he had cut in the rock. Then he rolled a great stone across the entrance of the tomb and went away.

The Guard at the Tomb
-Bethany, Golgotha, and the Praetorium-
Matthew 27:62-66
62 The next day (which is after the day of preparation) the chief priests and the Pharisees assembled before Pilate 63 and said, "Sir, we remember that while that deceiver was still alive he said, 'After three days I will rise again.' 64 So give orders to secure the tomb until the third day. Otherwise his disciples may come and steal his body and say to the people, 'He has been raised from the dead,' and the last deception will be worse than the first." 65 Pilate said to them, "Take a guard of soldiers. Go and make it as secure as you can." 66 So they went with the soldiers of the guard and made the tomb secure by sealing the stone.

Women Purchase and Prepare Burial Spices
Luke 23:55-56
55 The women who had accompanied Jesus from Galilee followed, and they saw the tomb and how his body was laid in it. 56 Then they returned and prepared aromatic spices and perfumes. On the Sabbath they rested according to the commandment.

The Stone Rolled Away
-Golgotha-
Matthew 28:2-4
2 Suddenly there was a severe earthquake, for an angel of the Lord descending from heaven came and rolled away the stone and sat on it. 3 His appearance was like lightning, and his clothes were white as snow. 4 The guards were shaken and became like dead men because they were so afraid of him.

Mary Magdalene Finds the Tomb Empty
-Golgotha-
John 20:1-2

1 Now very early on the first day of the week, while it was still dark, Mary Magdalene came to the tomb and saw that the stone had been moved away from the entrance. 2 So she went running to Simon Peter and the other disciple whom Jesus loved and told them, "They have taken the Lord from the tomb, and we don't know where they have put him!"

Peter, John and Mary Magdalene go to the Tomb
-Golgotha-
John 20:3-10

3 Then Peter and the other disciple set out to go to the tomb. 4 The two were running together, but the other disciple ran faster than Peter and reached the tomb first. 5 He bent down and saw the strips of linen cloth lying there, but he did not go in. 6 Then Simon Peter, who had been following him, arrived and went right into the tomb. He saw the strips of linen cloth lying there, 7 and the face cloth, which had been around Jesus' head, not lying with the strips of linen cloth but rolled up in a place by itself. 8 Then the other disciple, who had reached the tomb first, came in, and he saw and believed. 9 (For they did not yet understand the scripture that Jesus must rise from the dead.)

10 So the disciples went back to their homes.

Mary Magdalene Sees the Resurrected Jesus
-Golgotha-
Mark 16:9

9 Early on the first day of the week, after he arose, he appeared first to Mary Magdalene, from whom he had driven out seven demons.

John 20:11-17

11 But Mary stood outside the tomb weeping. As she wept, she bent down and looked into the tomb. 12 And she saw two angels in white sitting where Jesus' body had been lying, one at the head and one at the feet. 13 They said to her, "Woman, why are you weeping?" Mary replied, "They have taken my Lord away, and I do not know where they have put him!" 14 When she had said this, she turned around and saw Jesus standing there, but she did not know that it was Jesus.

15 Jesus said to her, *"Woman, why are you weeping? Who are you looking for?"* Because she thought he was the gardener, she said to him, "Sir, if you have carried him away, tell me where you have put him, and I will take him." 16 Jesus said to her, *"Mary."* She turned and said to him in Aramaic, "Rabboni" (which means Teacher). 17 Jesus replied, *"Do not touch me, for I have not yet ascended to my Father. Go to my brothers and tell them, 'I am ascending to my Father and your Father, to my God and your God."*

Mary Magdalene Returns to the other Disciples, but is not Believed
-Jerusalem-
Mark 16:10-11

10 She went out and told those who were with him, while they were mourning and weeping. 11 And when they heard that he was alive and had been seen by her, they did not believe.

The Other Women Come to the Tomb Nearing Sunrise
-Bethany and Golgotha-
Luke 24:1-7

1 Now on the first day of the week, at early dawn, the women went to the tomb, taking the aromatic spices they had prepared. 2 They found that the stone had been rolled away from the tomb, 3 but when they went in; they did not find the body of the Lord Jesus. 4 While they were perplexed about this, suddenly two men stood beside them in dazzling attire. 5 The women were terribly frightened and bowed their faces to the ground, but the men said to them, "Why do you look for the living among the dead? 6 He is not here, but has been raised! Remember how he told you, while he was still in Galilee, 7 that the Son of Man must be delivered into the hands of sinful men, and be crucified, and on the third day rise again."

Jesus Appearance to the Other Women
-Jerusalem-
Matthew 28:8-10

8 So they left the tomb quickly, with fear and great joy, and ran to tell his disciples. 9 But Jesus met them, saying, *"Greetings!"*

They came to him, held on to his feet and worshiped him. 10 Then Jesus said to them, *"Do not be afraid. Go and tell my brothers to go to Galilee. They will see me there."*

Report of the Solders to the Jewish Leaders
-Jerusalem-
Matthew 28:11-15

11 While they were going, some of the guard went into the city and told the chief priests everything that had happened. 12 After they had assembled with the elders and formed a plan, they gave a large sum of money to the soldiers, 13 telling them, "You are to say, 'His disciples came at night and stole his body while we were asleep.' 14 If this matter is heard before the governor, we will satisfy him and keep you out of trouble." 15 So they took the money and did as they were instructed. And this story is told among the Jews to this day.

The Women Tell the Apostles but They Do Not Believe
-Jerusalem-
Luke 24:8-11

8 Then the women remembered his words, 9 and when they returned from the tomb they told all these things to the eleven and to all the rest. 10 Now it was Mary Magdalene, Joanna, Mary the mother of James, and the other women with them who told these things to the apostles. 11 But these words seemed like pure nonsense to them, and they did not believe them.

Jesus Appears to two Disciples Traveling to Emmaus
-On the road to Emmaus-
(Mark 16:12-13)

12 After this he appeared in a different form to two of them while they were on their way to the country. 13 They went back and told the rest, but they did not believe them.

Luke 24:13-32

13 Now that very day two of them were on their way to a village called Emmaus, about seven miles from Jerusalem. 14 They were talking to each other about all the things that had happened. 15 While they were talking and debating these things, Jesus himself approached and began to accompany them 16 (but their eyes were kept from recognizing him). 17 Then he said to them, *"What are these matters you are discussing so intently as you walk along?"*

And they stood still, looking sad. 18 Then one of them, named Cleopas, answered him, "Are you the only visitor to Jerusalem who doesn't know the things that have happened there in these days?" 19 He said to them, *"What things?"* "The things concerning Jesus the Nazarene," they replied, "a man who, with his powerful deeds and words, proved to be a prophet before God and all the people; 20 and how our chief priests and rulers handed him over to be condemned to death, and crucified him. 21 But we had hoped that he was the one who was going to redeem Israel. Not only this, but it is now the third day since these things happened. 22 Furthermore, some women of our group amazed us. They were at the tomb early this morning, 23 and when they did not find his body; they came back and said they had seen a vision of angels, who said he was alive. 24 Then some of those who were with us went to the tomb, and found it just as the women had said, but they did not see him." 25 So he said to them, *"You foolish people – how slow of heart to believe all that the prophets have spoken! 26 Wasn't it necessary for the Christ to suffer these things and enter into his glory?"* 27 Then beginning with Moses and all the prophets, he interpreted to them the things written about himself in all the scriptures.

28 So they approached the village where they were going. He acted as though he wanted to go farther, 29 but they urged him, "Stay with us, because it is getting toward evening and the day is almost done." So he went in to stay with them.

30 When he had taken his place at the table with them, he took the bread, blessed and broke it, and gave it to them. 31 At this point their eyes were opened and they recognized him. Then he vanished out of their sight. 32 They said to each other, "Didn't our hearts burn within us while he was speaking with us on the road, while he was explaining the scriptures to us?"

Report of the Two Disciples to the Rest
-Jerusalem-
Luke 24:33-35

33 So they got up that very hour and returned to Jerusalem. They found the eleven and those with them gathered together 34 and saying, "The Lord has really risen, and has appeared to Simon!" 35 Then they told what had happened on the road, and how they recognized him when he broke the bread.

Jesus Appears to Ten of the Apostles
-Jerusalem, probably the Upper Room-
John 20:19a

19a On the evening of that day, the first day of the week, the disciples had gathered together and locked the doors of the place because they were afraid of the Jewish leaders.

Luke 24:36-43

36 While they were saying these things, Jesus himself stood among them and said to them, *"Peace be with you."* 37 But they were startled and terrified, thinking they saw a ghost. 38 Then he said to them, *"Why are you frightened, and why do doubts arise in your hearts? 39 Look at my hands and my feet; it's me! Touch me and see; a ghost does not have flesh and bones like you see I have."* 40 When he had said this, he showed them his hands and his feet. 41 And while they still could not believe it (because of their joy) and were amazed, he said to them, *"Do you have anything here to eat?"* 42 So they gave him a piece of broiled fish, 43 and he took it and ate it in front of them.

John 20:21-23

21 So Jesus said to them again, *"Peace be with you. Just as the Father has sent me, I also send you."* 22 And after he said this, he breathed on them and said, *"Receive the Holy Spirit. 23 If you forgive anyone's sins, they are forgiven; if you retain anyone's sins, they are retained."*

Thomas Still Does Not Believe
John 20:24-25

24 Now Thomas (called Didymus), one of the twelve, was not with them when Jesus came. 25 The other disciples told him, "We have seen the Lord!" But he replied, "Unless I see the wounds from the nails in his hands, and put my finger into the wounds from the nails, and put my hand into his side, I will never believe it!"

Jesus Appears to the Eleven Apostles
-Jerusalem, probably the Upper Room-
John 20:26-31

26 Eight days later the disciples were again together in the house, and Thomas was with them. Although the doors were locked, Jesus came and stood among them and said, *"Peace be with you!"* 27 Then he said to Thomas, *"Put your finger here, and*

examine my hands. Extend your hand and put it into my side. Do not continue in your unbelief, but believe." 28 Thomas replied to him, "My Lord and my God!" 29 Jesus said to him, *"Have you believed because you have seen me? Blessed are the people who have not seen and yet have believed."*

30 Now Jesus performed many other miraculous signs in the presence of the disciples, which are not recorded in this book. 31 But these are recorded so that you may believe that Jesus is the Christ, the Son of God, and that by believing you may have life in his name.

Jesus Appears to Seven Disciples
-Sea of Galilee-
John 21:1-14

1 After this Jesus revealed himself again to the disciples by the Sea of Tiberias. Now this is how he did so. 2 Simon Peter, Thomas (called Didymus), Nathanael (who was from Cana in Galilee), the sons of Zebedee, and two other disciples of his were together. 3 Simon Peter told them, "I am going fishing." "We will go with you," they replied. They went out and got into the boat, but that night they caught nothing.

4 When it was already very early morning, Jesus stood on the beach, but the disciples did not know that it was Jesus. 5 So Jesus said to them, *"Children, you don't have any fish, do you?"* They replied, "No." 6 He told them, *"Throw your net on the right side of the boat, and you will find some."* So they threw the net, and were not able to pull it in because of the large number of fish.

7 Then the disciple whom Jesus loved said to Peter, "It is the Lord!" So Simon Peter, when he heard that it was the Lord, tucked in his outer garment (for he had nothing on underneath it), and plunged into the sea. 8 Meanwhile the other disciples came with the boat, dragging the net full of fish, for they were not far from land, only about a hundred yards.

9 When they got out on the beach, they saw a charcoal fire ready with a fish placed on it, and bread. 10 Jesus said, *"Bring some of the fish you have just now caught."* 11 So Simon Peter went aboard and pulled the net to shore. It was full of large fish, one hundred fifty-three, but although there were so many, the net was not torn. *12 "Come, have breakfast,"* Jesus said. But none of the disciples dared to ask him, "Who are you?" because they knew it was the Lord. 13 Jesus came and took the bread and gave it to

them, and did the same with the fish. 14 This was now the third time Jesus was revealed to the disciples after he was raised from the dead.

Jesus Reinstates Peter
-Sea of Galilee-
John 21:15-25

15 Then when they had finished breakfast, Jesus said to Simon Peter, *"Simon, son of John, do you love me more than these do?"* He replied, "Yes, Lord, you know I love you." Jesus told him, *"Feed my lambs."* 16 Jesus said a second time, *"Simon, son of John, do you love me?"* He replied, "Yes, Lord, you know I love you." Jesus told him, *"Shepherd my sheep."* 17 Jesus said a third time, *"Simon, son of John, do you love me?"* Peter was distressed that Jesus asked him a third time, "Do you love me?" and said, "Lord, you know everything. You know that I love you." Jesus replied, *"Feed my sheep. 18 I tell you the solemn truth, when you were young, you tied your clothes around you and went wherever you wanted, but when you are old, you will stretch out your hands, and others will tie you up and bring you where you do not want to go."* 19 (Now Jesus said this to indicate clearly by what kind of death Peter was going to glorify God.) After he said this, Jesus told Peter, *"Follow me."*

20 Peter turned around and saw the disciple whom Jesus loved following them. (This was the disciple who had leaned back against Jesus' chest at the meal and asked, "Lord, who is the one who is going to betray you?") 21 So when Peter saw him, he asked Jesus, "Lord, what about him?" 22 Jesus replied, *"If I want him to live until I come back, what concern is that of yours? You follow me!"* 23 *So the saying circulated among the brothers and sisters that this disciple was not going to die. But Jesus did not say to him that he was not going to die, but rather, "If I want him to live until I come back, what concern is that of yours?"*

24 This is the disciple who testifies about these things and has written these things, and we know that his testimony is true.

25 There are many other things that Jesus did. If every one of them were written down, I suppose the whole world would not have room for the books that would be written.

Jesus Also Appeared to More Than Five Hundred
1st Corinthians 15:6

6 Then he appeared to more than five hundred of the brothers and sisters at one time, most of whom are still alive, though some have fallen asleep.

The Great Commission
-A Mountain in Galilee-
Matthew 28:16-20

16 So the eleven disciples went to Galilee to the mountain Jesus had designated. 17 When they saw him, they worshiped him, but some doubted. 18 Then Jesus came up and said to them, *"All authority in heaven and on earth has been given to me. 19 Therefore go and make disciples of all nations, baptizing them in the name of the Father and the Son and the Holy Spirit, 20 teaching them to obey everything I have commanded you. And remember, I am with you always, to the end of the age."*

Mark 16:16-18

16 "The one who believes and is baptized will be saved, but the one who does not believe will be condemned. 17 These signs will accompany those who believe: In my name they will drive out demons; they will speak in new languages; 18 they will pick up snakes with their hands, and whatever poison they drink will not harm them; they will place their hands on the sick and they will be well."

Jesus Appears to His Disciples in Jerusalem
-Jerusalem-
Luke 24:44-49

44 Then he said to them, *"These are my words that I spoke to you while I was still with you, that everything written about me in the Law of Moses and the prophets and the psalms must be fulfilled."* 45 Then he opened their minds so they could understand the scriptures, 46 and said to them, *"Thus it stands written that the Christ would suffer and would rise from the dead on the third day, 47 and repentance for the forgiveness of sins would be proclaimed in his name to all nations, beginning from Jerusalem. 48 You are witnesses of these things. 49 And look, I am sending you what my Father promised. But stay in the city until you have been clothed with power from on high."*

Acts 1:3-8

3 To the same apostles also, after his suffering, he presented himself alive with many convincing proofs. He was seen by them

over a forty-day period and spoke about matters concerning the kingdom of God. 4 While he was with them, he declared, "Do not leave Jerusalem, but wait there for what my Father promised, which you heard about from me. 5 For John baptized with water, but you will be baptized with the Holy Spirit not many days from now."

6 So when they had gathered together, they began to ask him, "Lord, is this the time when you are restoring the kingdom to Israel?" 7 He told them, *"You are not permitted to know the times or periods that the Father has set by his own authority. 8 But you will receive power when the Holy Spirit has come upon you, and you will be my witnesses in Jerusalem, and in all Judea and Samaria, and to the farthest parts of the earth."*

The Ascension of Jesus
-The Mount of Olives, near Jerusalem-
Luke 24:-50

50 Then Jesus led them out as far as Bethany, and lifting up his hands, he blessed them.

Acts 1:9-11

9 After he had said this, while they were watching, he was lifted up and a cloud hid him from their sight. 10 As they were still staring into the sky while he was going, suddenly two men in white clothing stood near them 11 and said, "Men of Galilee, why do you stand here looking up into the sky? This same Jesus who has been taken up from you into heaven will come back in the same way you saw him go into heaven."

Luke 24:52-53

52 So they worshiped him and returned to Jerusalem with great joy, 53 and were continually in the temple courts blessing God.

Matthias Chosen to Replace Judas
-Jerusalem, probably the Upper Room-
Acts 1:12-26

12 Then they returned to Jerusalem from the mountain called the Mount of Olives (which is near Jerusalem, a Sabbath day's journey away). 13 When they had entered Jerusalem, they went to the upstairs room where they were staying. Peter and John, and James, and Andrew, Philip and Thomas, Bartholomew and Matthew, James son of Alphaeus and Simon the Zealot, and Judas son of James were there. 14 All these continued together in prayer

with one mind, together with the women, along with Mary the mother of Jesus, and his brothers. 15 In those days Peter stood up among the believers (a gathering of about one hundred and twenty people) and said, 16 "Brothers, the scripture had to be fulfilled that the Holy Spirit foretold through David concerning Judas – who became the guide for those who arrested Jesus – 17 for he was counted as one of us and received a share in this ministry." 18 (Now this man Judas acquired a field with the reward of his unjust deed, and falling headfirst he burst open in the middle and all his intestines gushed out. 19 This became known to all who lived in Jerusalem, so that in their own language they called that field Hakeldama, that is, "Field of Blood.") 20 "For it is written in the book of Psalms, 'Let his house become deserted, and let there be no one to live in it,' and 'Let another take his position of responsibility.' 21 Thus one of the men who have accompanied us during all the time the Lord Jesus associated with us, 22 beginning from his baptism by John until the day he was taken up from us – one of these must become a witness of his resurrection together with us." 23 So they proposed two candidates: Joseph called Barsabbas (also called Justus) and Matthias. 24 Then they prayed, "Lord, you know the hearts of all. Show us which one of these two you have chosen 25 to assume the task of this service and apostleship from which Judas turned aside to go to his own place." 26 Then they cast lots for them, and the one chosen was Matthias; so he was counted with the eleven apostles.

The Holy Spirit Comes at Pentecost
-Jerusalem, probably the Upper Room-
See Note: Pentecost
Acts 2:1-13

1 Now when the day of Pentecost had come, they were all together in one place. 2 Suddenly a sound like a violent wind blowing came from heaven and filled the entire house where they were sitting. 3 And tongues spreading out like a fire appeared to them and came to rest on each one of them. 4 All of them were filled with the Holy Spirit, and they began to speak in other languages as the Spirit enabled them.

5 Now there were devout Jews from every nation under heaven residing in Jerusalem. 6 When this sound occurred, a crowd gathered and was in confusion, because each one heard them speaking in his own language. 7 Completely baffled, they said,

"Aren't all these who are speaking Galileans? 8 And how is it that each one of us hears them in our own native language? 9 Parthians, Medes, Elamites, and residents of Mesopotamia, Judea and Cappadocia, Pontus and the province of Asia, 10 Phrygia and Pamphylia, Egypt and the parts of Libya near Cyrene, and visitors from Rome, 11 both Jews and proselytes, Cretans and Arabs – we hear them speaking in our own languages about the great deeds God has done!" 12 All were astounded and greatly confused, saying to one another, "What does this mean?" 13 But others jeered at the speakers, saying, "They are drunk on new wine!"

Peter Address the Crowd
-Jerusalem-
Acts 2:14-41

14 But Peter stood up with the eleven, raised his voice, and addressed them: "You men of Judea and all you who live in Jerusalem, know this and listen carefully to what I say. 15 In spite of what you think, these men are not drunk, for it is only nine o'clock in the morning. 16 But this is what was spoken about through the prophet Joel: 17 'And in the last days it will be,' God says, 'that I will pour out my Spirit on all people, and your sons and your daughters will prophesy, and your young men will see visions, and your old men will dream dreams. 18 Even on my servants, both men and women, I will pour out my Spirit in those days, and they will prophesy. 19 And I will perform wonders in the sky above and miraculous signs on the earth below, blood and fire and clouds of smoke. 20 The sun will be changed to darkness and the moon to blood before the great and glorious day of the Lord comes. 21 And then everyone who calls on the name of the Lord will be saved.'

22 "Men of Israel, listen to these words: Jesus the Nazarene, a man clearly attested to you by God with powerful deeds, wonders, and miraculous signs that God performed among you through him, just as you yourselves know – 23 this man, who was handed over by the predetermined plan and foreknowledge of God, you executed by nailing him to a cross at the hands of Gentiles. 24 But God raised him up, having released him from the pains of death, because it was not possible for him to be held in its power. 25 For David says about him, 'I saw the Lord always in front of me, for he is at my right hand so that I will not be shaken. 26 Therefore my heart was glad and my tongue rejoiced; my body also will live

in hope, 27 because you will not leave my soul in Hades, nor permit your Holy One to experience decay. 28 You have made known to me the paths of life; you will make me full of joy with your presence.'

29 "Brothers, I can speak confidently to you about our forefather David, that he both died and was buried, and his tomb is with us to this day. 30 So then, because he was a prophet and knew that God had sworn to him with an oath to seat one of his descendants on his throne, 31 David by foreseeing this spoke about the resurrection of the Christ, that he was neither abandoned to Hades, nor did his body experience decay. 32 This Jesus God raised up, and we are all witnesses of it. 33 So then, exalted to the right hand of God, and having received the promise of the Holy Spirit from the Father, he has poured out what you both see and hear. 34 For David did not ascend into heaven, but he himself says, 'The Lord said to my lord, "Sit at my right hand 35 until I make your enemies a footstool for your feet."' 36 Therefore let all the house of Israel know beyond a doubt that God has made this Jesus whom you crucified both Lord and Christ."

37 Now when they heard this, they were acutely distressed and said to Peter and the rest of the apostles, "What should we do, brothers?" 38 Peter said to them, "Repent, and each one of you be baptized in the name of Jesus Christ for the forgiveness of your sins, and you will receive the gift of the Holy Spirit. 39 For the promise is for you and your children, and for all who are far away, as many as the Lord our God will call to himself." 40 With many other words he testified and exhorted them saying, "Save yourselves from this perverse generation!" 41 So those who accepted his message were baptized, and that day about three thousand people were added.

The Fellowship of the Believers
Acts 2:42-47

42 They were devoting themselves to the apostles' teaching and to fellowship, to the breaking of bread and to prayer. 43 Reverential awe came over everyone, and many wonders and miraculous signs came about by the apostles. 44 All who believed were together and held everything in common, 45 and they began selling their property and possessions and distributing the proceeds to everyone, as anyone had need. 46 Every day they continued to gather together by common consent in the temple

courts, breaking bread from house to house, sharing their food with glad and humble hearts, 47 praising God and having the good will of all the people. And the Lord was adding to their number every day those who were being saved.

All of this happened over two thousand years ago and Jesus is still seeking those who haven't yet accepted Him as their personal Saviour.

Here are some facts you need to consider

It is a fact that God loves you: John 3:16 says: "For this is the way God loved the world. He gave his one and only Son, so that everyone who believes in him will not perish but have eternal life."

It is a fact that you are a sinner: Romans 3:23 says: "For all have sinned and fall short of the glory of God."

It is a fact that there is no one that is innocent: Romans 3:10-18 says: "There is no one righteous, not even one, there is no one who understands, there is no one who seeks God. All have turned away; together they have become worthless; there is no one who shows kindness, not even one. Their throats are open graves; they deceive with their tongues, the poison of asps is under their lips. Their mouths are full of cursing and bitterness. Their feet are swift to shed blood, ruin and misery are in their paths, and the way of peace they have not known. There is no fear of God before their eyes."

It is a fact that sin leads to death: Romans 6:23 says: "For the payoff of sin is death, but the gift of God is eternal life in Christ Jesus our Lord."

It is a fact that Christ died for you: Romans 5:8 says: "But God demonstrates his own love for us, in that while we were still sinners, Christ died for us."

It is a fact that you must confess Jesus as Lord. Romans 10:9 says: "If you confess with your mouth that Jesus is Lord and believe in your heart that God raised him from the dead, you will be saved."

It is a fact that you can know that you are now saved. Romans 10:13 says: "For everyone who calls on the name of the Lord will be saved."

It is a fact that you can now have peace with God. Romans 5:1 says: "Therefore since we have been declared righteous by faith, we have peace with God through our Lord Jesus Christ."

It is a fact that you are no longer under condemnation. Romans 8:1 says: "There is therefore now no condemnation for those who are in Christ Jesus. Because of Jesus' death on our behalf, we will never be condemned for our sins if you have trusted in Him."

It is a fact that your faith in Jesus has set you free. Romans 8:2 says: "For the law of the life-giving Spirit in Christ Jesus has set you free from the law of sin and death."

It is a fact that nothing can separate you from the love of God. Romans 8:38-39 says: "For I am convinced that neither death nor life, neither angels nor demons, neither the present nor the future, nor any powers, neither height nor depth, nor anything else in all creation, will be able to separate us from the love of God that is in Christ Jesus our Lord."

Now is the time, if you haven't already done it, to pray and ask Jesus to forgive your sins, be the Lord of your life and give you the salvation He has already provided through His death and resurrection.

Would you like to follow the Romans Road to salvation? If so, here is a simple prayer you can pray to God. Saying this prayer is a way to declare to God that you are relying on Jesus the Christ for your salvation. The words themselves will not save you. Only faith in Jesus can provide salvation! "God, I know that I have sinned against you and am deserving of punishment. But Jesus took the punishment that I deserve so that through faith in Him I could be forgiven. With your help, I place my trust in You for salvation. Thank You for Your wonderful grace, your forgiveness and the gift of eternal life! Amen!"

Your next step is to find a church where the Pastor is preaching and teaching the whole truth from the bible and giving alter calls for salvation.

Notes

Blasphemy Against the Holy Spirit
Blasphemy against the Holy Spirit is when something of God is credited to the Devil
Read Matthew 9:32-34, Matthew 12:22-24, Luke 11:14-15 and Mark 3:22-30

10 And everyone who speaks a word against the Son of Man will be forgiven, but the person who blasphemes against the Holy Spirit will not be forgiven.

Empty

The following scriptures are not in The Nestle's Greek New Testament one of the most reliable available today.

Matthew 18:11 For the Son of man is come to save that which was lost. (KJV)

Matthew 23:14 Woe unto you, scribes and Pharisees, hypocrites! For ye devour widows' houses, and for pretense make long prayer: therefore, you shall receive the greater damnation. (KJV)

John 5:4 For an angel went down at a certain season into the pool, and troubled the water: whosoever then first after the troubling of the water stepped in was made whole of whatsoever disease he had. (KJV)

Jairus' Daughter

There are three accounts about the death of Jairus' daughter dying. Matthew 9:18 states that his daughter has just died but Mark 5:23 and Luke 8:42 say that she is near death or dying.

Matthew simplified the account by saying she had already died. The end result of the three accounts is the same. She died before Jesus could get to her as recorded in Mark 5:35 and Luke 8:49.

Jericho

There are three different, but similar, accounts of blind men being healed at Jericho. Matthew says there were two men, Mark and Luke say there was one man.

Luke says they were approaching Jericho, Matthew says they were leaving, and Mark says in Mark 10:46a "Then they came to Jericho. As Jesus and his disciples, together with a large crowd were leaving the city." It would seem they came and left at the same time. Orville E. Daniel, author of A Harmony of the Four Gospels, states "Apparently He was leaving Old Jericho and was on his way to the new city built by Herod the Great."

Because of all these facts I believe that Mark and Luke are the same event and Matthew is a totally different one. This clears up an apparent contradiction. Also when Jesus was at Jericho he had an encounter with Zacchaeus, Luke 19:1-10, probably in the new city of Jericho.

Jesus Anointed
There were three different recorded events of Jesus being anointed. The first was by a sinful woman, Luke 7:36-50. The second was six days before the Passover, John 12:1-11. The third time was two days before the Passover, Matthew 26:1-13 and Mark 14:1-11.

Jesus' Half Brothers and Sisters
Matthew 12:46-47, 13:55 Mark 3:31-32, 6:3 Luke 8:19-21 John 7:3 Acts 1:14 1Cor. 9:5 Gal 1:19

It is very clear from Scripture that Mary had other children after Jesus. Matthew and Mark list the names of the four other sons of Mary as James, Joseph (Joses), Simon and Judas. Mark also includes the statement that Mary had daughters. The evidence of Scripture clearly indicates that Mary had at least six other children after the birth of Jesus.

Jesus brothers and probably sisters did not receive salvation until after the resurrection of Jesus.

Also it strongly appears that two books of the Bible were written by two of Jesus brothers, James (the book of James) and Judas (the book of Jude).

Judas Iscariot
It appears that when Jesus passed the bread and cup to the disciples, for what we call communion, that Judas was already gone. John 13:27-30

Pentecost
There was about one hundred and twenty gathered in the upper room when the Holy Spirit came on the day of Pentecost and all of them, including the women and Mary the mother of Jesus and his brothers were filled with the Holy Spirit and spoke in tongues. Acts 1:14-15 and Acts 2:4

Peter's Denials
Jesus told Peter that he would deny him three times; Matthew 26:31-35, Mark 14:27-31, and Luke 22:31-34.

It stands to reason when Peter was being questioned about knowing Jesus that more than one person was questioning him in each of the three denials. Each time he was questioned he responded, but it was still only three different events.

Court of Annas

1st Denial: Matthew 26:69-70, Mark 14:66-80a, Luke 22: 54-57 and John 18:15-18

Courtyard of Caiaphas

2nd Denial: Matthew 26:71-72, Mark 14:68b-70a, Luke 22:58 and John 18:25

3rd Denial: Matthew 26:73-75, Mark 14:70b-72, Luke 22:59-62 and John 18:26-27

The Disciples of Jesus

This is by no means the complete list of all the disciples that Jesus had. I believe that the only reason they are mentioned by name is because they were also chosen as Apostles. Even the events of when all the Apostles were called first as disciples is not recorded. We only have seven out of twelve that are recorded as to when they were called. At one point Jesus sent out seventy two, Luke 10:1, disciples ahead of him to every town and place where he was about to go.

1st Event

John 1:35-42

John though to be the son of Zebedee and younger brother of James - first encounter

Simon Peter brother of Andrew - first encounter

Andrew brother of Simon Peter - first encounter

(Note) It appears the first time these three disciples encountered Jesus they only stayed with him for a short time and went back to their fishing trade. John 1:39

2nd Event

John 1:43-51

Philip of Bethsaida

Nathanael (Bartholomew)

3rd Event

Matthew 4:18-22 Mark 1:16-20

Simon Peter brother of Andrew - second encounter

Andrew brother of Simon Peter - second encounter

James son of Zebedee and older brother of John - first encounter

John son of Zebedee and brother of James - second encounter

(Note) Again it appears that three of these four disciples went back to fishing. Only Andrew remained with Jesus.

4th Event

Luke 5:1-11

Simon Peter brother of Andrew - third encounter

James son of Zebedee and older brother of John - second encounter

John son of Zebedee and younger brother of James - third encounter

(Note) This time these three disciples left everything and stayed with Jesus. It appears from Luke 5:10 that Peter, James and John were not only fishermen but were partners in a fishing business. It took the large catch of fish to convince them to leave there business and stay with Jesus.

5th Event - The calling of Matthew

Mark 2:13-14

Matthew (Levi) of Capernaum

The Triumphal Entry

Matthew 21:2 says that there were two animals. Mark 11:2, Luke19:30 and John 12:14 mention only one colt. Even though Mark, Luke and John apparently didn't see the need to mention the donkey and only mentioned the colt, Robert L. Thomas, the author of A Harmony of the Gospels, states, "The mother of the colt was probably led in front to make the colt more at ease in carrying its first rider."

The Apostles of Jesus

Matthew 10:1-4 Mark 3:16-19 Luke 6:12-16 Acts 1:12-26

1. Simon Peter brother of Andrew
2. James son of Zebedee and older brother of John
3. John son of Zebedee and brother of James
4. Andrew brother of Simon Peter
5. Philip of Bethsaida
6. Matthew (Levi) of Capernaum
7. Thomas (Didymus)
8. James the younger son of Alphaeus
9. Simon the Zealot (the Canaanite)
10. Nathaniel (Bartholomew)
11. Thaddaeus (Judas) son of James

12. Judas Iscariot - Iscariot probably means the man from Kerioth
13. Matthias (chosen to replace Judas Iscariot) Acts 1:12-26)

The Two Demoniacs

Matthew 8:28-34 clearly states there were two demon-possessed men. Mark 5:1-20 and Luke 8:26-39 only refer to one. One conclusion about this is that one of the men was the leader and more prominent. My conclusion is that maybe only one of the two men was delivered because Jesus said clearly said in Mark 8, *"Come out of that man, you unclean spirit"*.

The Visit of the Magi

When the Magi found Jesus he was in Nazareth not in Bethlehem. Luke 2:39 is clear that Joseph and Mary returned to Nazareth after they had done everything required by the Law of the Lord. See Leviticus 12:1-8

Made in the USA
Middletown, DE
11 April 2018